THE ARCHERS' COUNTRY COOKBOOK

Mollie Harris plays the part of Martha Woodford in the B.B.C.'s celebrated and much loved serial *The Archers*. The character she plays is that of an ordinary country woman – just what Mollie is in real life. She was one of a poor family of seven children and spent the first twenty years of her life in the tiny village of Ducklington in Oxfordshire. She acquired her cooking skills by watching and helping her mother cook for the large family.

Mollie is also well known for her country cookery series on *Pebble Mill At One*. She has for several years been a regular contributor on country topics to many television and radio programmes and is the author of a number of popular books about life in Oxfordshire in the 1920s and 1930s.

The Archers' Country Cookbook

MARTHA WOODFORD

With decorations by
Val Biro

ARROW BOOKS

Arrow Books Limited
3 Fitzroy Square, London W1P 6JD

An imprint of the Hutchinson Publishing Group

London Melbourne Sydney Auckland
Wellington Johannesburg and agencies
throughout the world

First published by Hutchinson 1977
Arrow edition 1979

Made and printed in Great Britain
by The Anchor Press Ltd
Tiptree, Essex

ISBN 0 09 920910 1

CONTENTS

CONTENTS

May 83

June

CONTENTS

INTRODUCTION

Living in a small community like Ambridge where everybody knows everybody else, there are very few secrets amongst us, especially when it comes to folks' eating habits. Doris Archer has only to mention in the shop how much she and Dan enjoyed a new recipe for pig's liver, and before you can blink an eye half the village housewives have begged the know-how from her.

That's how it is in a close-knit village like ours, we're for ever swopping new and old recipes or passing on ideas as to how we might improve some of them, simply by adding or taking away – perhaps a little spice, or a sprinkling of herbs, a squeeze of lemon or an extra egg.

Over the years I have collected hundreds of good, homely, country recipes, sticking them into scrapbooks just as they were handed to me. Some quickly scribbled on the back of an envelope at a Women's Institute meeting, or maybe dotted down in between serving groceries in the shop. In our haste maybe we have left out one of the ingredients, but if the dish turns out all right, then we have created yet another recipe. Most of mine originated from country homes, they have been a way of life for most of the village folk. But when the new-comers come to live in Ambridge they bring with them their own special recipes. Mrs Laura Archer brought New Zealand delicacies, young Pat Archer from Wales has introduced us to several tasty Welsh dishes, while Jean Harvey who came from the London area brought into our lives a touch of what she calls 'high living'.

But most of the recipes in this book are the real old ones that have been handed down from one generation to another, with alterations over the years according to the whim or taste of the housewife, or in some cases because of the financial state of the family; the old adage 'cut your coat according to your cloth' has changed many a recipe which years ago might have read 'take a dozen eggs' to something simpler but still nourishing and tasty, though not so expensive.

Well, I thought it was time I shared with you some of the contents of my scrap cookbooks. So here is a selection of them which can be used throughout the seasons. They are, on the whole, simple to follow and not expensive to produce, and I hope that housewives everywhere will find them useful, interesting and, above all, tasty and nourishing.

Most of the recipes give 4 good servings. Where they give more, or less, you'll find that I say so at the end of the recipe. All spoon measures are level unless otherwise stated.

TABLES OF WEIGHTS
AND MEASURES

METRIC CONVERSION TABLE

Weight	*Liquid capacity*
1 oz = 25 grammes	1 fluid oz = 25 millilitres
2 oz = 50 grammes	2 fluid oz = 50 millilitres
4 oz = 100 grammes	5 fluid oz = 150 millilitres
8 oz = 225 grammes	8 fluid oz = 225 millilitres
12 oz = 325 grammes	10 fluid oz = 300 millilitres
16 oz (1 lb) = 450 grammes	15 fluid oz = 450 millilitres
1½ lb = 700 grammes	20 fluid oz (1 pint) =
2 lb = 900 grammes	600 millilitres
	2 pints = 1200 millilitres

SPOON MEASURES

1 oz syrup = 1 level tablespoon
1 oz granulated sugar = 2 level tablespoons
1 oz icing sugar = 3 level tablespoons
1 oz flour = 2 level tablespoons
1 oz fat = 2 level tablespoons
1 oz suet = 3 level tablespoons

JANUARY

Throughout most of January the cold east wind whips through the village like a sharp knife, and flurries of snow darken the cold winter sky. The children come home from school, scrabbling noisily from the bus and soon set about snowballing, while the little ones chant to the falling snowflakes "Tis Old Mother Juggins, picking her geese, selling her feathers a penny a piece'. Most of the menfolk work on the farms or big estates and have been out in the cold weather most of the day. The country housewife will see that she has a good casserole or hot soup filled with nourishing vegetables waiting for him and the rest of the family when they come home on these chill winter evenings.

If you have an electric blender like Jill Archer has, you can prepare soups in half the time. I make a great many during the cold days and Joby will often take some in his flask instead of coffee for his midmorning drink.

Here are three of his favourites.

Mother's mixture
(a hot nourishing soup)

1 leek	3 peppercorns
2 large onions ⎫ peeled	1 blade mace
1 large carrot ⎭	1 pint bacon stock or water
1 oz beef dripping	1 tablespoon cornflour
Salt and pepper	1 gill milk
1 teaspoon mixed dried herbs (thyme and marjoram)	1 tablespoon chopped parsley

Slice the leek, onions and carrot finely. Put the dripping in the saucepan, and when hot add all the vegetables, fry for 3 minutes without browning. Add salt, pepper, mixed herbs, peppercorns, mace and the liquid and cook for 30 minutes. Mix the cornflour with milk and add to the soup, cook for another 2 minutes stirring all the time. Sprinkle chopped parsley on top just before serving. (A tablespoon of cream added with the parsley makes the soup much nicer.)

Onion soup

6 medium sized onions	Salt and pepper to taste
2 oz butter or dripping	¼ pint milk
1 pint water or stock made from meat bones, poultry or game	A little grated cheese

Peel and chop the onions finely, place them along with the fat into a saucepan and cook for 3 minutes, stirring all the time. Add stock or water and cook until onions are tender. Add salt and pepper. Boil the milk and add to the stock. Serve with grated cheese and croutons.

Croutons can be made easily. Use any stale bread, brown or white. Cut the bread, crust free, into small squares about ¼″ thick and fry in bacon fat till golden brown. Cool and keep in a closed tin until needed.

This soup is an excellent pick-me-up.

Mixed vegetable soup

1 lb vegetables made up of carrots, celery, potato, onion and leek, with the emphasis on the onion
1 oz dripping

Salt and pepper to taste
1 dessertspoon chopped parsley
1½ pints stock or water
A little cornflour for thickening

Clean and peel the vegetables and chop up quite small. Melt the dripping in the saucepan, add the vegetables and cook for about 10 minutes, stirring all the time. Add the salt and pepper, parsley and stock. Simmer for about 30 minutes until all the vegetables are cooked. If you want a thick soup, just mix a level tablespoon of cornflour or plain flour with a little cold water, stir till smooth and then add to the soup.

This is one of Joby's favourite dishes, and young Neil, who came to us from the big city, reckoned it was a meal fit for a king, so I renamed it 'King's casserole'. Sometimes on cold days, he would have two or three helpings of it. But I never minded as long as it did him good.

King's casserole

¾ lb stewing beef, cut into cubes

¼ lb ox kidney, cut in pieces

2 tablespoons plain flour

Salt and pepper to taste

¾ lb onions, peeled and sliced

2 carrots, peeled and sliced

2 meat cubes

*1 teaspoon chopped parsley

*1 teaspoon chopped thyme

¾ pint stock or water

For the dumplings

¼ lb self-raising flour

Pinch salt

2 oz suet, grated

About 2 tablespoons of water

Place the flour on a plate and season well with the salt and pepper. Dip the steak and kidney into this, flouring each piece well. Now place the meat into a good sized casserole, add the peeled, sliced onions and carrots. Sprinkle the meat cubes over, and add the herbs and tip in any of the seasoned flour left on the plate. Add the stock or water so that the contents of the casserole are just covered, and put on the lid. Place in a pre-heated over, middle shelf (Gas 3, 335°F) and cook for 3 hours.

Now make up the dumplings. Put the flour, salt and grated suet into a bowl; add the water, mixing with the hand, to make a stiffish dough. Roll into balls about the size of an egg and drop them into the casserole. Cook for a further ½ hour, stirring them once to push the dumplings down into the gravy. Serve hot with plenty of green vegetables.

When we have King's casserole I make it a potato-less day. You have all the nourishment in the dumplings and the lovely thick stew.

*Dried can be used, but if so remember you only need half the quantity otherwise the flavour would be much too strong.

Ethel's belly pork

It's funny, as you go through life, you pick up recipes and hints in the queerest of places. For years I was never quite sure how to really cook belly pork, so that it was nice and tender. Then one day I was on the bus coming home from shopping and the two women sitting in front of me were talking about cooking, and one of them was talking in a very loud voice about her husband's favourite meal, belly pork. And she was telling her friend, and the rest of the passengers, how she cooked it. So I made a mental note of what she said and have used it ever since, always referring to it as 'Ethel's belly pork'.

3 strips belly pork
Salt and pepper
2 meat cubes
2 good sized onions, sliced

3 good sized potatoes, sliced
$\frac{1}{2}$ cup water
Knob of dripping

Lay the belly pork in a meat tin, season well, add the meat cubes crumbled small. Cover with the sliced onion then the sliced potatoes. Pour the water over the top and dot the potatoes with good beef dripping. Cover and cook in a moderate over (Gas 4, 355°F) for about an hour. Remove the cover and cook for a further $\frac{1}{2}$ hour to crisp up the potatoes. Lovely served with Brussels sprouts.

Stuffed breast of lamb

Two dishes that can be served at the same meal are stuffed breast of lamb and stuffed onions (turn to page 28 for the recipe) save about a third of the stuffing for the onions.

While you have the oven on for the breast of lamb and onions, why not put in a few potatoes to bake at the same time? On the bottom shelf you could cook a milk pudding, leaving just your cabbage or Brussels to cook on the top of your cooker.

1 breast of lamb (or mutton)
1 oz dripping

Stuffing

4 oz fresh breadcrumbs
1 teaspoon mixed herbs
  (parsley, thyme and
  marjoram)

1 small onion, chopped
1 egg
Salt and pepper to taste

Ask the butcher to bone the breast, or do it yourself, using a small sharp knife. Use the bones later for stock or soup.

Mix together the breadcrumbs, herbs and onion and bind with a beaten egg. Flatten out the breast of lamb and spread the stuffing mixture over it. Roll up neatly and secure with a skewer and then tie with string. Spread on the dripping, and place in a baking tin to cook for 2 hours at Gas 4, 355°F.

It there is any of the stuffed breast of lamb left over, a slice or two cold between bread makes a hearty lunch for a working man (10 o'clock break).

Sometimes after a pheasant shoot Mr Woolley will sell off, to the locals, birds that have been shot about too much to send to market. Or maybe the birds are old and here again would not be suitable for sale in the butchers' shops. Mr

Woolley knows that I will always buy one or two of these off him, and this is how I cook an old pheasant.

Pheasant casserole

1 pheasant	1 medium onion sliced
1 oz flour	1 oz mushrooms
Salt and pepper	1 teaspoon each parsley and
1 oz dripping	thyme
1 oz streaky bacon	1 pint stock or water
	1 gill red wine (home-made)

First pluck and draw the bird. Of course, plucking any sort of bird is hard work if you don't know how, but the easiest way to do it is to lay it on its back and hold it by the legs with the left hand. Then plunge the right thumb and forefinger as far into the thick feathers as you can so that you can feel the skin, and then begin to pluck out the down and feathers together, pulling the feathers away from the neck and working towards the legs. When you have removed all the feathers (don't bother about the head), you are now ready to 'draw' the bird. Lay it on its back and with a sharp knife cut off the head, then cut off the neck close to the body (keep the neck for gravy making along with the giblets). Now draw out the crop and windpipe from the hole that you made when cutting off the neck. Turn the bird over so that its rear end faces you, make the vent opening bigger with a sharp knife, put your hand inside the bird and draw out its insides. Discard the entrails but keep the liver, heart and gizzard. I always put the bird under the tap at this stage and this washes out any blood, then wipe it out with a clean tea towel. Put the neck, liver and heart into salt water to soak for a while. Cut the gizzard open and turn out any food and peel off the coarse skin, wash well and add to the rest of the giblets.

Cut the bird into joints and dip each one in the seasoned flour. Melt the dripping in a frying pan and fry each joint lightly on both sides for a few minutes, then place in the bottom of a casserole. Chop the bacon small and toss this in the frying pan for a few moments then tip bacon over the joints. Now fry the onion lightly and add to the casserole along with the mushrooms and herbs and any seasoned flour that is left. Add the stock and wine, covering the contents. Put on the lid and cook for 2–3 hours at Gas 3, 335°F.

Doris Archer's rabbit pie

On account of Joby's job as forrester, land owners and clients who come to order wood or young saplings, often bring him a brace of partridge or pheasant, or maybe a couple of rabbits or hare. So we do very well when it comes to game. We keep our own hens too, and when they get old and have finished laying they make us tasty meals; and then Joby always rears a few cockerels as well, specially for our own use, so we don't go hungry.

Here is Doris Archer's recipe for a super rabbit pie and one that we often have for Sunday dinner.

Rough puff pastry

1 lb plain flour	6 oz lard
Salt	Water
6 oz butter or margarine	Squeeze of lemon juice

Pie filling

1 rabbit, jointed	½ lb mushrooms, chopped
1 oz flour, seasoned	1 tablespoon parsley
½ lb streaky bacon, chopped	Pepper and salt
1 onion, sliced	Gravy stock (made from boiled bones)

To make the pastry, sift the flour and salt into a bowl and cut the fat into ½″ cubes. Add to the flour. Mix to a stiff dough with cold water to which a squeeze of lemon has been added.

Flour the pastry board and róll the dough to an oblong about ½" thick. Brush off any loose flour and fold the pastry into three, lightly pressing the edges together. Give the pastry a half turn, roll again and fold as before. Put in a cold place for 20 minutes to rest. Then roll and fold a further twice more with two more rests, always brushing off loose flour before folding.

Dip the rabbit pieces into the seasoned flour and place some in the bottom of a pie dish. Alternate with layers of chopped streaky bacon, onion, mushrooms and parsley. Season with salt and pepper and add enough gravy stock to cover. Place a pie funnel in the middle of the pie dish.

Flour the pastry board and roll out the pastry. Cut long strips and place round the dampened rim of the pie dish, then completely cover the top with a good layer of pastry. Crimp the edges. Brush with egg or milk and cook in a hot oven (Gas 7, 425°F) for ¼ hour and then reduce to Gas 3, 335°F for a further hour. To prevent the crust from burning cover with foil.

If you don't want to make such a big rabbit pie as mine, then use half the ingredients. But, hot or cold, it makes a lovely meal and Joby will always finish any left over from dinner for his supper.

We are very fond of parsnips, either boiled as an ordinary vegetable or part boiled and then slipped in with roast beef to finish cooking. But one day Nora and I were chatting about parsnips and she came up with this lovely idea of frittered parsnips and they really are super.

Frittered parsnips—Irish style

5 parsnips
1 tablespoon flour
1 egg

Salt and pepper
Little dripping or lard

Peel parsnips, cut up small and place in cold salted water and cook until tender. Strain well, mash and stir in the flour, egg, salt and pepper. Form into small cakes with a wooden spoon and fry in hot fat on both sides till golden brown.

Stuffed onions

Peel the onions and cook them whole in salted water for $\frac{1}{2}$–$\frac{3}{4}$ hour. Scoop out the centres, chop and mix with remaining stuffing from the breast of lamb (see page 23). Fill the onion shells and bake in a moderate oven (Gas 4, 355°F) for about 30 minutes until brown on top.

Never throw stale bread away, there are dozens of recipes in which breadcrumbs are used; you'll find several in this book. Simply grate any stale bread, the breadcrumbs can be kept for a while in polythene bags, or stored in a freezer either in containers or polythene bags.

If you use bread when baking tartlets for filling later, don't throw the bread away, just put the pieces between greased proof paper and crush with a milk bottle. Store the crumbs in an airtight container, you will find them useful when frying fish etc. in egg and breadcrumbs.

Here's a nice light pudding, using up stale bread:

Bread and butter pudding

6 slices white bread (crustless)	2 eggs
2 oz butter	1 pint milk
6 oz mixed dried fruit	2 oz caster sugar
1 oz demerara sugar	A drop of vanilla essence

Spread the butter quite thickly on the bread, cutting the slices in half to fit in the dish. Butter a dish and put in layer of bread and butter. Mix the dried fruit and demerara sugar together and sprinkle some of this over the bread. Continue like this till all the bread, butter and fruit is used up, finishing with a layer of bread and butter. Beat eggs well, stir in the milk, sugar and vanilla essence. Pour this over the bread. Bake in warm oven (Gas 4, 355°F) for about 40 minutes, so that the pudding is golden brown.

Treacle tart

Another recipe which a demonstrator at a W.I. meeting gave us, again using up breadcrumbs and is very easily made.

6 tablespoons golden syrup	*Shortcrust Pastry*
1 tablespoon black treacle	8 oz self raising flour
Juice and grated rind of	4 oz margarine
1 lemon	1 oz lard
Pinch nutmeg	1 egg
5 heaped tablespoons white	
breadcrumbs	

Make the pastry, roll it out and line a greased plate with it. Warm the syrup, treacle and rind and juice of lemon and nutmeg in a saucepan. Remove from heat and stir in bread-crumbs. Pour the mixture over the pastry, make a lattice pattern over top with thin strips of pastry made from the bits left over and bake in a hot oven (Gas 7, 425°F) until pastry is golden brown.

Jill Archer's coconut and cherry chew

Jill Archer comes up with some lovely recipes, especially when we hold our Birthday meeting of the W.I. each year. You see she was a cookery demonstrator before she married Mr Phil, so she really knows about cooking. At the last birthday do she produced what she called 'A coconut and cherry chew'. Everybody said how lovely it was and we were all asking for the recipe. My word didn't I sell a lot of coconut and glacé cherries for a few days afterwards! I reckon we nearly all had a go at making it, even Mary Pound made some and she's not often taken up with fancy cooking.

	Topping
6 oz plain flour	2 egg whites
Pinch of salt	1 tablespoon caster sugar
3 oz butter or margarine	2 tablespoons coconut
3 oz castor sugar	1 dozen glacé cherries
1 egg yolk	Heaped tablespoon chopped nuts

Grease a flat, Swiss roll type tin. Put the flour in a bowl along with the salt and the butter and sugar. Rub the butter in with the fingertips until the mixture looks like fine bread-crumbs, now add the egg yolk and stir it in. Tip this mixture into your greased tin and press it down lightly with the palm of the hand. Now whip together the egg whites, the caster sugar and coconut. Spread this over the mixture in the tin. Dot the cherries on the top and then sprinkle on the nuts.

Bake in a preheated oven (Gas 4, 355°F) for about 20–25 minutes until the topping is a light golden brown. Mark out in squares but do not remove from the tin until cold.

I make at least one sort of wine almost every month of the year, and sometimes even two or three sorts in high summer. But I draw the line in December, because I've neither the time nor the space.

Wine should never be made with young parsnips, young carrots, or potatoes. All these vegetables must be mature before using for wine making. So January, February and March are the best months for making wine with these.

Parsnip wine

4 lb parsnips
1 gallon water
2 lemons

2 oranges
4 lb demerara sugar (3lb for dry wine)
½ oz yeast

Scrub parsnips clean, but do not peel. Cut into chunks, place in a large saucepan along with the water and the sliced unpeeled lemons and oranges and cook until the parsnips are tender but not mushy. Strain the liquor onto the sugar and stir well with a wooden spoon. When cool, but not cold, sprinkle on the yeast (or do it the old-fashioned way by spreading the yeast on a piece of toast and placing it on the top of the wine). Cover the wine with a thick cloth and leave for 10 days. Strain into a demijohn and fix air-lock on top. Leave until all working has ceased. Then bottle off and try not to drink it until it has stood for a year. Well, if you make it in January you could try it next Christmas!

February fill dyke often lives up to its reputation as a wet and windy month. But we do have the odd sunny day which reminds us that, although we have some nasty weather ahead, spring is not so far away. Already our robin (I call him our robin because it seems to be the same one that comes back year after year) is singing his merry song as he sits in the bright yellow forsythia bush alongside our kitchen window. We've got crocus and aconites blooming in the garden, and now that the nights are drawing out, my Joby likes to get on with a bit of digging when he comes home in the evening. He loves his garden and has already planted his shallots.

But with the damp weather there's still the need for hot, warming meals during the dark days of February.

This is a very nourishing soup, easily made, and a lovely flavour – especially if you use bacon water instead of plain water.

Thick pea soup

½ packet (½ lb) dried peas
3 pints bacon stock or water
1 medium sized turnip, peeled and chopped
4 carrots, peeled and chopped

2 onions, finely sliced
Pepper and salt
1 tablespoon medium oatmeal

Soak the peas overnight – the instructions are on the packet. Strain and boil up the next day with the 3 pints of stock or water, cook until tender. Strain the peas, keeping the liquid, and mash to form a paste. Put them back into the liquid, and add the peeled chopped turnip, carrot and finely sliced onion, salt and pepper to taste. Simmer gently till the vegetables are cooked, stirring often. Mix the oatmeal with a little cold water to a paste and add to the saucepan and simmer again for a few minutes. (A teaspoon of dried mint improves the flavour; add this just before serving.)

Pat Archer's leek and cheese soup

½ lb leeks
1 oz butter or dripping
Salt and pepper to taste

1 pint stock or water
4 oz grated cheese

Here's a recipe that young Pat Archer gave me when she first came to Ambridge. I often make it for supper on Saturday nights during the winter-time and it sends you to bed real warm.

Top and tail the leeks and wash them well in cold salted water. Drain and cut them into thinish slices. Melt the fat in the frying pan and toss in the leeks and cook gently for about 8 minutes, moving them round the pan all the while. Tip into a saucepan, add the pepper and salt and the stock or water and simmer until the leeks are tender (about 20 minutes). Add the grated cheese *after* you have dished up the soup, or give each person a small dish of grated cheese separately so that they can add it as they wish.

You will notice that I often say use *stock* for soups. This can be made from any bones (including chicken) which you boil up along with a pint of water to a lb of bones. Often the butcher will be glad to let you have some. Good stock can also be made from the water that a joint of bacon has been cooked in-never ever throw that away. 'Course if you chuck in a few root vegetables like carrots, onions or parsnips, and herbs, this will make a very flavoursome stock.

A nice tasty breakfast treat

Bacon
Slices of bread
A little margarine

A few thin slices of cheese
1 egg, beaten

After you have fried your breakfast bacon, leave the fat in the pan. Then make these sandwiches by simply cutting slices of bread, spreading them with margarine, putting slivers of cheese between and pressing together. Dip the sandwiches (both sides) in the beaten egg and fry in the bacon fat, turning once, until they are golden brown. (This makes one egg go quite a long way.)

Oxfordshire clanger
(boiled bacon pudding)

For the crust	For the filling
½ lb plain flour	4–6 oz bacon, cut in chunks
¼ lb suet	(collar or shoulder)
Good pinch salt	½ teaspoon mixed herbs
½ teaspoon mixed herbs	1 good sized onion
Water to mix	Salt and pepper

Mix all crust ingredients together well to make a stiffish workable dough. Flour board and place dough on it and press with the flat of the hand into an oblong shape. Dot bacon all over the dough, sprinkle on herbs, cover with finely sliced onion, season with salt and pepper and roll up pudding into a roly poly. Well flour a pudding cloth, place pudding on and roll up, sewing it up to seal. (Foil may be used instead of a pudding cloth.) Put into a saucepan of boiling water and cook for 3–3½ hours. Serve with carrots and Brussels sprouts. No need for potatoes with this nourishing bacon pudding. Remember that the water in the saucepan will need topping up several times while the pudding is cooking.

During the coming weeks I shall probably get the chance of some pigeons. You see, around this time of the year George Barford has what he calls a vermin shoot when they kill grey squirrels, pigeons, jay and anything else that he calls vermin. He knows how fond we are of pigeon and always brings me some. One day when he sailed into the shop with some, he told me that someone had shot a couple of jays. When I asked him what he was going to do with them he said, 'Oh, just chuck um away.' So I asked him for them. 'Whatever are you going to do with um,' he enquired? 'Have um stuffed,' I told him. And that's just what we did. We took them over to a mate of Joby's who stuffs birds and things just as a hobby. He made a real good job of the jays, they're such pretty birds. He put them into a glass case with bits of moss and foliage and they look lovely on my sideboard. Visitors think they are Victorian and are quite surprised when I tell them that they are modern.

Anyway, here are a couple of ways of cooking wood pigeons.

Jugged pigeons

2 pigeons	1 tablespoon flour, seasoned
2 streaky rashers	with salt and pepper
1 oz dripping	Water
2 good sized onions, sliced	1 meat cube
Half a dozen sage leaves	

Pluck the birds, take out the insides (if you're not sure how to do this turn to the recipe for pheasant casserole on page 25) and cut them through lengthways. Cut the bacon into small pieces and fry in the dripping. Place the bacon at the bottom of the casserole, now fry the onions and sage leaves and add this to the onions. Dip the halves of pigeons into the seasoned flour and fry lightly on both sides until they are browned. Lay the pigeons in the casserole, cover with the remaining fat and add any seasoned flour that is left. Pour in enough warm water so that the birds are just covered, crumble over the meat cube. Cover and cook slowly for 2–3 hours at Gas 3, 335°F.

Stuffed baked pigeons

Young pigeons bake nicely and make a tasty meal, especially if you stuff them with sage and onion stuffing.

2 or 3 young pigeons
Salt and pepper

About 4 rashers streaky
  bacon
Dripping

For the stuffing
4 oz breadcrumbs
1 onion, chopped
6 or 8 sage leaves, chopped
  finely

Salt and pepper to taste
1 oz dripping
1 egg (to bind)

Pluck and draw the birds and wash out with water. Mix all the stuffing ingredients together. Rub the pigeons with a little salt and pepper and stuff insides. Wrap streaky rashers round the birds, fixing them with wooden cocktail sticks, dot with dripping and bake in a moderate oven (Gas 4, 355°F) for about an hour.

Soused herrings

Herrings
Salt and pepper
Water

Vinegar
2 or 3 bayleaves

Scrape the scales from the herrings, cut off their heads, clean out the insides and place them in a fireproof dish. Add the pepper and salt, cover with equal quantities of water and vinegar and add the bay leaves. Cover the dish with foil and cook for about ½ hour in a moderate oven (Gas 4, 355°F).

Mrs Perkins always puts about 4 cloves in with her herrings when she cooks them, but my Joby doesn't care for the flavour that the cloves give, so I don't bother with them. But it's just a matter of taste.

Walter Gabriel always reckons that it's an onion a day that keeps the doctor away. If that's the case Joby and me should be as fit as fleas, for we have onions, one way or another, most days.

Braised sliced onions

1 oz margarine or dripping   Salt and pepper
3 good sized onions, peeled

Melt the fat in a pan, slice the onions and toss into the pan along with salt and pepper. Cook for 2–3 minutes, transfer to a fireproof dish and cook in the oven at Gas 3, 335°F for about an hour.

Leek pasty

I really don't know where I got this recipe for leek pasty. All I know is, it's very tasty and my Joby loves it, especially when I put some in for his ten o'clock break.

For the pastry
6 oz plain flour
Pinch of salt
1 egg
2½ oz butter or margarine

For the filling
2–3 lb leeks, boiled and
    chopped up roughly
3 oz grated cheese
½ apple, sliced

Mix flour and pinch of salt in a bowl. Cut the fat into small pieces and rub into the flour with the fingertips until it looks

41

like fine breadcrumbs. Add egg, and a little water if necessary, to mix into a firm dough. Flour a pastry board very lightly and roll out the pastry with light, quick rolls. Lightly grease a sandwich tin and line it with the pastry. Leave it to stand in a cool place for $\frac{1}{4}$–$\frac{1}{2}$ hour. (This stops it from getting tough or from shrinking when you cook it)

Fill the bottom of the flan case with leeks, sprinkle with cheese, add a few slices of apple and season to taste. Cover with the rest of the pastry, crimp edges, brush with milk and bake in a hot oven (Gas 7, 425°F) for 20–30 minutes until pastry is golden brown. Serve hot or cold.

Shrove Tuesday nearly always falls in February but we have pancakes quite often for pudding. I make the mixture before I go to work, because the pancakes will be much lighter if the mixture can be made a few hours before it's cooked. We just have them with lemon juice and sugar on Shrove Tuesday, but other times we have hot syrup or honey or jam in them, and they are super filled with stewed apple and the pancakes topped with thick cream, just as a special treat. Of course, they can be filled with all sorts of savouries too. The pancake mixture is the same whatever the filling. A lovely savoury filling can be made by mashing a large cooked potato and mixing it with 2 oz each of chopped ham and cream (or grated) cheese, an egg yolk and a tablespoon of chopped parsley. Gently warm the mixture in a saucepan for a few minutes, then place in the pancake and roll up.

Pancakes for pancake day

4 oz plain flour
1 egg

$\frac{1}{3}$ pint milk to make a fairly
thin batter
Lard for frying

Beat the pancake mixture together until the batter bubbles. Leave to stand for at least an hour. Put a knob of fat into the frying pan and heat until light blue smoke rises. Give the pancake mixture a quick whisk, then cover the frying pan base with a thin coating of the batter. When nicely brown, turn carefully and cook the other side. This is when you should toss them, when they are cooked. I always toss ours, and Joby usually rather nervous in case I should miss catching the pancake on the way down – so far I've been lucky.

Fruit cake

This is what I call a good standby cake because it keeps well for a couple of weeks or more. I usually have one on the go and one in the cake tin in case I haven't any time to make cakes for Joby's lunch tins.

8 oz margarine
6 oz caster sugar
1 good tablespoon golden
  syrup
1 good tablespoon semolina

3 eggs
6 oz mixed dried fruit
12 oz self-raising flour
A little milk

Cream margarine and sugar until light and fluffy. Beat in the syrup, semolina, eggs and fruit. Fold in the flour, and enough milk to make a soft dropping consistency. Then line a cake tin with greaseproof paper, tip ingredients and bake in a moderate oven (Gas 4, 355°F) for $1–1\frac{1}{4}$ hours. Test by pushing knife into centre, if the blade comes out clean then the cake is done; if not, cook for another 5–10 minutes. Cool on rack.

Polly's Swiss roll

When Polly gave me this simple recipe for a Swiss roll, she
said it was the easiest thing in the world to make, and so it is.

2 eggs   2 oz self-raising flour
2 oz caster sugar   Jam for filling

Whisk the eggs and sugar together until frothy, fold in the
flour with a metal spoon. Line a Swiss roll tin with greaseproof paper and pour in the mixture. Put into a preheated
oven (Gas 4, 355°F) and cook on the middle shelf for 10–12
minutes. While the Swiss roll is cooking gently warm the
jam. When the Swiss roll is cooked, spread on the warm jam
straight away and roll up quickly. (The greaseproof paper
lining makes this very easy.) Best eaten the same day.

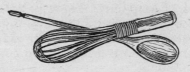

Polly's brownies

'Here you are,' Polly said to me the other afternoon, 'don't
say I never give you anything.' And she handed me a small
paper bag over the counter. 'I've been making Lucy some
cakes,' she went on, 'Brownies she calls them. Apparently
she had some at a little friend's birthday party the other week
and she's been worrying me ever since to make some, and do
you think I could find how to make them in any book that
I've got? No, I had to wait to ask Lucy's friend's mummy
for the recipe. I thought you could have one with your afternoon cup of tea, Martha.' So as soon as Polly had done her
bit of shopping I put the kettle on for me afternoon cuppa

and tried one of her brownies and they were smashing. I wondered why I hadn't come across them before.

2 oz unsweetened chocolate	4 oz self-raising flour
3 oz margarine	Pinch of salt
5 oz caster sugar	2 tablespoons chopped
2 eggs	nuts

First put the chocolate and the margarine in a basin over a saucepan of hot water. When they have melted beat in the sugar and the eggs and then fold in the flour and salt. Tip the chopped nuts in and stir well. Grease a flat meat tin and spread the mixture evenly over it and cook in a pre-heated oven (Gas 4, 355°F) for about 35 minutes. Leave to cool for a few moments before cutting the cake into squares, leave in the tin until quite cold.

You can spread a little chocolate icing on the top if you wish. Just mix 2 tablespoons of icing sugar and 1 tablespoon of drinking chocolate together with a drop of water to make a smooth paste. Dip a knife in hot water and then spread the icing over the squares, and drop a Smartie sweet on each.

Last year Sid left his carrots in the ground all the winter. Come February when he started digging, he wanted them out of the way; they were in good shape because of the mild winter. He happened to mention in the shop that he was going to chuck them on to the compost heap. I told him to bring them along to me and I'd soon make some wine with them. You must have mature carrots for wine making, and here's what you do.

Carrot wine

Scrub and clean 4 lb carrots (don't peel them), and slice them quite finely. Put into a saucepan containing 1 gallon cold water and 2 oz root ginger. Boil until the carrots are tender. Put 4 lb demerara sugar into a large container (not metal) and pour the *strained* carrot liquor over the sugar, add 1 oz yeast and the juice of 2 oranges and 2 grapefruit. Cover with a cloth and leave the wine in a warm place to work for about a week or 10 days. Strain into a demijohn, fix the air lock and leave until all working has stopped. Bottle off and leave for 8–10 months before drinking.

MARCH

I can't believe that it's March already, it doesn't seem five minutes ago that it was the start of a new year, but you've only got to look at our garden to realize that spring is just around the corner, for our Polyanthus flowers are a picture; every colour of the rainbow they are, but I notice that the blessed sparrows are pecking at the petals, little devils! I feed them all winter and that's all the thanks I get.

Jethro came rushing into the shop today, covered from head to foot in brown March dust he was. He told me that up at Brookfield they've been working non-stop to get the rest of the planting done, and by the look of him he'd brought half the field with him.

'Give us a couple a they bottles of that lemonade tack,' he said, 'I dun't reckon as I could spit a tanner I be that dry.'

'Do you know you're quite a wealthy man,' I said to him. 'You've heard what they says about March dust being worth a king's ransom.'

'That be damned fer a tale,' he replied. 'You wants to hear what my Lizzie calls it when 'er has to wash me filthy overalls. You'd a laughed t'other day, Martha, I go's indoors for me dinner and my Lizzie hardly recognized me, I was as black as a tinker; 'course our Clarrie was thur and her started singing "Mammy". You see I'd had me goggles on while we was planting and when I took um awf I'd got two great white rings round me eyes. My Lizzie said I looked like

49

Al Jolson. Oh, and her said I was to ask you if you kept such things as little cartons of carraway seeds, we got her sister a-coming over and her do love a bit of seedy cake.'

''Course I got carraway seeds,' I told him, 'but I shall expect Lizzie's recipe for seed cake, it might be a bit different to the one that I use.'

Off he went saying that he would pop the recipe in one day when he was passing the shop – if he remembered to ask his wife for it.

Here's my leek and potato soup recipe. Goodness knows where I got it from, but I've been using it for ages and it's ever so nourishing and makes you warm all over when you've had a bowl full of it.

Leek and potato soup

4 good size leeks	Salt and pepper to taste
1 oz dripping	1 tablespoon chopped mint
1 pint stock	(or one teaspoon of dried)
1 large potato	¼ pint milk

Wash the leeks well in cold water, then cut them up into about 1" lengths. Put the dripping into a saucepan, add the leeks and cook for about 10 minutes, stirring often. Now add the stock. Grate up the raw potato and add salt and pepper and tip this into the saucepan and cook for about 20 minutes. Stir in the chopped mint and add the milk just before serving.

There's nothing so warming on a cold windy day as a good steak and kidney pudding that's been cooking all morning. Mrs Doris Archer told me the other day that when they were farming at Brookfield, they often had one for Sunday dinner. I must say my Joby and me likes a roast always on a Sunday no matter what the weather. Anyhow, here's Doris's recipe, but I think it's the one that most folks use, though my mother always put a sprinkling of mixed herbs in hers.

Steak and kidney pudding

Crust
8 oz self-raising flour   3–4 oz grated suet
Pinch salt   Water to mix

Filling for the pudding
¾ lb stewing steak (I always   1 meat cube
  ask for pudding beef)   1 chopped onion
4 oz kidney   Stock or water
1 tablespoon flour, salt and pepper

Put the flour and salt into bowl then add the grated suet. Mix with a little cold water to a nice soft, but not too sticky, dough. Tip out on to a floured board and press lightly with the palm of the hand till the dough is about ¼″ thick. Grease a pudding basin and line it with three parts of the dough, leaving enough for a lid.

Cut the meat up into cubes. Put the tablespoon of flour, salt and pepper on a plate and roll each piece of meat in it. Crumble a meat cube and put in the bottom of the dough-lined basin. Now add the meat and the chopped onion until the basin is full. Cover the contents with stock or water. Now put on the lid, first wetting the edges so that it seals the pudding down. Cover either with greased paper or foil and tie down. Half fill a saucepan with boiling water, put the basin in, bring the water up to the boil then turn down so that it's just a steady boil. Top up with water often as you will find it will boil away quite quickly. Cook the pudding for at least three hours. Serve with Brussels sprouts, carrots or swede and boiled potatoes, but if you are watching your weight forget the potatoes for once.

Baked liver
(how Joby's mum cooked it)

One day, soon after me and Joby got married, I started to clear out the attic in our cottage. 'Course Joby had been living there for some time and there was a rare collection of stuff pushed up there out of the way. Well, amongst the boxes of clothes and crockery I found his mother's old cookery book. All the recipes were handwritten in a sort of exercise book, with a piece of linen stuck over the cover to make it firm. There are some lovely recipes in it, and some of course I shall never be able to try out because I'd never be able to get all the ingredients. But others I find ever so handy and we often have a meal that I call 'One of your mum's specials'. Joby likes to think that I sometimes use a recipe from that old cook book and he says that I'm nearly as good a cook as his mother was. This is one of his favourites.

¾ lb pigs liver, sliced	A little salt
1 tablespoon flour, pepper and salt	A little dripping
	1 beef cube
2 good sized onions	¼ cup boiling water
2 or 3 large potatoes	

Mix the pepper and salt together with the flour and dip each slice of liver in it, covering both sides. Lay the liver in a baking dish. Now peel and slice the onions and cover the liver with them. Peel and slice the potatoes (quite thick), place them over the onions and sprinkle with a little salt. Dot the potatoes with a few knobs of dripping and crumble the meat cube over too. Now pour the boiling water over the potatoes, just dropping a few drops on each. Put a lid on the baking dish and cook in a warmish oven (Gas 4, 355°F) for about 1 hour. Take off the cover and cook for a further ½ hour to crisp up the potatoes.

Mind you, I had to work out the gas and electric temperature for cooking the liver dish and all the others that I use from that old book for that matter. In the original liver recipe it just said 'get your fire going well and the oven fairly warm.'

Prue Forrest's oxtail stew

Prue Forrest is what I call a good homely cook. With Tom coming in at all hours when he was 'keepering' all those years she needed to cook meals that wouldn't spoil if they were not eaten at once. She found one of the nicest and handiest dishes was a tasty oxtail stew. This is one of their favourite meals in the wintertime and a bit different to the one that I found in Joby's mum's cook book. Adding the haricot beans to the traditional recipe is a super idea and makes the stew even more nourishing.

1 tablespoon flour
Salt and pepper to taste
1 oxtail, cut up
¾ lb onions, peeled and sliced
1 clove (optional)
2 peppercorns
¼ lb streaky bacon rashers

½ lb turnips
½ lb carrots
1 teaspoon chopped parsley
Stock or water
½ lb haricot beans (soaked in cold water the night before they are needed)

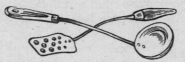

Put half of the flour on a plate and mix it with the salt and pepper. Dip each joint into the seasoned flour and put them in a good sized casserole. Add the peeled, sliced onions, the clove and peppercorns. Now cut up the bacon into small pieces and peel and slice the carrots and turnips and add all this to the casserole. Sprinkle on the chopped parsley and fill up the casserole with stock or water. Cook in a slow oven (Gas 3, 335°F) for 4–5 hours. Now mix the rest of the flour with a few spots of cold water, then add this to the casserole, and put it back in the oven to cook for a further 30 minutes. Now strain off the water from the haricot beans and put them into a saucepan, cover with fresh cold water and simmer gently for about ½ hour until they are nice and soft. Strain and add the beans to the cooked oxtail a few minutes before serving.

Serve this stew with potatoes baked in their jackets (page 57). – unless of course you are one of those folks who wouldn't dream of eating it with anything other than plain boiled potatoes!

At this time of the year George Barford and Gordon Armstrong have a day or two culling the wild ducks that come and settle on the lake on Mr Woolley's estate, and they often give Joby a couple. We love wild duck, they are so much more flavoursome than the ordinary domestic kind. We don't like any game that has been 'hung' because it makes it taste rather strong, so I cook them within 2 or 3 days of being killed, but again it's just a matter of taste.

Roast wild duck

When I've plucked and drawn my wild ducks (and if you're not sure how to do this turn to the recipe for pheasant casserole on page 25) this is how I stuff them.

Stuffing

2 oz breadcrumbs	Salt and pepper
1 good sized grated onion	1 oz dripping
2 teaspoons chopped sage	1 egg

Mix this all together, binding well with the egg. Stuff this into the tail end of the duck filling up the cavity. Rub salt over the body, fold the wings tidily behind the bird and set it in a baking tin. Cover with knobs of dripping and cook in a preheated oven (Gas 5, 380°F) and bake for about 1½ hours, basting often.

While this is cooking make the gravy. First rinse the salt water from the giblets, then place them into a saucepan. Bring up to the boil and cook until soft. Add a little salt to taste. Blend a spoonful of cornflour with a little cold water, add this to the giblets and stir until it thickens.

Savoury fish cutlets

2 cutlets of cod or hake
½ lb tomatoes (bottled or tinned ones can be used)

Salt and pepper to taste
1 oz butter
1 tablespoon flour
1 teaspoon milk

Grease a baking dish and cover the bottom with half the sliced tomatoes, then place the cutlets on the top and cover with the rest of the tomatoes. Add pepper and salt and dot with butter. Cover the dish with foil and cook in a hot oven (Gas 6, 400°F) for about 20 minutes. Drain off the liquid and put aside. Put a little butter into a saucepan, mix the flour with the spoonful of milk, add the drained off liquid that the fish was cooked in and bring up to the boil. This will make a lovely sauce to cover the fish with before serving.

I was telling Mary Pound the other day how well our leeks have turned out this time and that I had made some lovely leek and potato soup and she said, 'Ah, but have you ever tried leeks cooked in a casserole along with potatoes and bacon?'

'No, I haven't,' I said, but if she was to give me the recipe there and then, blow me if I wouldn't try it instead of the soup, just for a change. And you can take my word for it, its very tasty, even my Joby liked it so it must have been nice. He usually says he don't like new things that I try out on him, he likes the old-fashioned meals that he's always been used to.

Mary Pound's leek casserole

2 large potatoes	½ lb rashers
4 leeks	2 teaspoons parsley
A little dripping for frying	Stock or water
Salt and pepper to taste	

Peel and slice the potatoes. Wash the leeks and slice them and fry them and the potatoes in the dripping. Put a layer of potato into a casserole and then a layer of leeks and season well. Cut the rashers up into small pieces and add these and cover with the chopped parsley. Now add the rest of the leeks and finish off with the remaining potatoes. Pour in the stock or water so that it half fills the casserole. Put the lid on and cook in a moderate oven (Gas 5, 380°F) for about ¾ hour, then remove the lid, dot with a little dripping and cook for a further 15 minutes until the potatoes are brown.

Potatoes baked in their jackets

You can cook these at the same time as the Oxtail stew and the bread pudding.* Choose big potatoes, allowing one or two for each person depending on their appetites. Scrub them well and prick them all over with a fork. Place in the oven on the bottom shelf. After they have been cooking for about

*You will find the recipe for oxtail stew on page 53, and the bread pudding on page 60.

$1\frac{1}{2}$ hours, turn them over to cook for another hour. You can tell if the potatoes are done by pressing them with the finger and thumb when they should feel quite soft.

Working in the village shop like I do, I meet all sorts of folk. One minute I might be joking and laughing about with Harry Booker or Nora, and the next being nice and polite to someone like Mrs Harvey or Mrs Tregorran. Not that either of them come in regular like, but when they want something special in a hurry and haven't got time to go into the town, they'll pop in to see if I stock it.

Take the other day. In come Mrs Tregorran, ''Morning Martha,' she said, 'I wonder if you have such a thing as a carton of cottage cheese and some black grapes?'

'Well, as a matter of fact I have got cottage cheese,' I told her, 'quite a lot of people in the village buy it from me, regular, but I don't ever get asked for black grapes. What was it you wanted them for?' I asked.

'I have someone rather special coming for a meal tonight and I thought I would make one of my cheese cakes. You remember,' she went on, 'I made one for the harvest supper last year. The grapes are simply for decoration, still I can use mandarins instead, you do have mandarins I suppose?'

Well, off she went with a tin of mandarins and the cottage cheese, but not before she had promised to let me have the recipe for her special harvest cheese cake. Not that I should make it very often, just for me and Joby, but it would be nice to have it all the same. Anyhow Mrs Tregorran said that it keeps ever so well in a freezer, if you cut it up in slices and wrap each one separately in foil.

So I made one on Sunday and it turned out beautiful; mind you my Joby only had one slice, he said that it was too sickly for him, but I love it and I could eat it till the cows come home. But I've got to think of me figger, so I put about half of it into the shop freezer and I gets a slice out just when I fancy and takes it home for my pudding. So here's the recipe, its a bit fiddling to do, but worth all the time you spend making it.

Carol Tregorran's cheese cake

For the crust

$\frac{1}{2}$ lb digestive biscuits	3 oz unsalted butter

For the filling

3 tablespoons cold water	2 eggs
$\frac{1}{2}$ oz powdered gelatine	4 oz caster sugar
8 oz cottage cheese	Pinch salt
4 oz fresh cream cheese	Juice of an orange
Rind of a lemon, finely grated	$\frac{1}{4}$ pint double cream

First crush the biscuits up finely. (I did this by putting them between two layers of greaseproof paper and then rolling them with a milk bottle.)

Put the butter into a saucepan and melt over a low heat. Stir in the crushed biscuit crumbs to absorb all the butter. Now press this mixture over the base of a loose bottomed cake or flan tin and put into the fridge to chill while you are preparing the cheesecake mixture. Put the water into a small saucepan and sprinkle in the gelatine and set it aside to soak for a few minutes. Rub the cottage cheese through a coarse sieve into a large basin (or break it up with a fork). Now add the cream cheese and the finely grated lemon rind and mix well. Separate the eggs. Add half the sugar to the egg yolks and the salt and beat until creamy and fluffy. Now gently heat the pan with the gelatine in, stirring all the while, but do not let it boil. Take off the heat once it has dissolved and add the strained orange juice to it, then whisk this into the egg yolks and then blend all this into the cheese mixture. Whisk the egg whites until thick, add the remaining sugar and whisk again until stiff. Fold this and the lightly whipped cream into the cheese mixture. Pour into the chilled cake base, smooth level on the top and chill in the fridge for about 3 hours. Decorate with segments of mandarins (or halved black grapes) or leave plain, just as the fancy takes you.

Old-fashioned bread pudding

You could cook this old-fashioned bread pudding at the same time as you cooked the oxtail stew (see page 53 for the recipe). The oven temperature needed is about the same, but of course the pudding doesn't take as long as the casserole.

About 1 lb stale bread	2 heaped teaspoons mixed
6 oz mixed dried fruit	pudding spice
4 oz sugar	4 oz suet or margarine
	2 eggs, beaten

Soak the stale bread in hot water for about an hour. Then take the bread out of the water and squeeze it as dry as you can and put it into a mixing bowl. Now add the dried fruit, sugar, spice and suet (or margarine). Mix it all up well with the hand, and then add the beaten eggs. The mixture should now be quite wet and sloppy. Grease a meat tin and tip all the mixture into it. Cook for 1½–2 hours in a slow oven (Gas 3, 335°F) until nicely browned on the top. Lovely eaten hot or cold.

Peggy Archer's tea-time toffee tart

Peggy Archer is another jolly good cook and we often have a chat in the shop about cooking. The other day she said to me 'Martha, I don't think that the younger generation ever bother to spend half a day bread and cake making as we did, and in your case still do. I remember when Tony and Jennifer and Lilian used to come home from school they were always hungry, and on my special baking days they would come rushing in, having caught a whiff of the lovely smell of the bread baking, and they would sit down and eat hot bread rolls straight from the oven. I used to tell them that they would have indigestion, but they wouldn't take the slightest notice. 'Oh they were lovely growing up days for them,' she said, 'they hadn't a care in the world then.'

She gave me this recipe for toffee tart ages ago, it makes a nice pudding at this time of the year when most of us have used up all the apples and a lot of the bottled fruit.

For the pastry
6 oz self-raising flour
2 oz lard or margarine
2 oz sugar
A little milk and water to mix

For the filling
½ lb finely chopped dates
2 dessertspoons golden syrup
2 tablespoons porridge oats
1 oz margarine

First of all make the pastry in the usual way. Roll it out and line a greased sandwich tin with it. In a separate bowl mix up the dates, syrup, oats and margarine together. Cover the pastry with this mixture and bake in a warmish oven (Gas 6, 400°F) second from top for about ½ hour.

Lizzie Larkin's seed cake

Jethro Larkin was as good as his word and a few days after he had been into the shop for the carraway seeds, he popped in again and gave me his Lizzie's recipe for seedy cake. Mind you old Walter always called it fly cake. I suppose the seeds do look a bit like little flies when you come to think of it. Anyhow here's how Lizzie makes her cake. The difference between her recipe and the one that I have always used is just that she mixes brown sugar and a few carraway seeds together and sprinkles it on the top of the mixture before she bakes it. I tried this and liked it, it gave the cake a nice sweet crispy, crusty top.

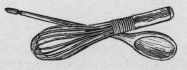

8 oz self-raising flour	3 eggs and a little milk, well beaten
Pinch salt	
4 oz margarine	1 tablespoon demerara sugar and 1 teaspoon caraway seeds mixed for topping
6 oz caster sugar	
1 dessertspoon caraway seeds	

Put the flour, salt, and margarine into a mixing bowl and rub the ingredients together with the finger tips until it looks like breadcrumbs. Now add the sugar and the caraway seeds and the eggs that have been well beaten with the milk. Line a cake tin with greaseproof paper and turn the cake mixture into it. Sprinkle the top with the demerara sugar and caraway seeds. Place in a preheated oven (Gas 4, 355°F) for about 1–1¼ hours. When cooked leave for a few minutes before taking the paper off, then cool on a cake rack.

Cheese scones

I reckon cheese scones are one of the easiest things to make and sometimes when I think that there's not much left in the cake tins for my Joby's lunch I rub up a few. Mind you I like them piping hot, straight out of the oven, split and spread with butter, but Joby likes them best left whole, and cold. They take no longer than 12 minutes to make and cook, and there's not many recipes quicker than this one.

6 oz self-raising flour
Pinch of salt
1 flat teaspoon dry mustard
½ flat teaspoon cayenne
    pepper

2 oz margarine
3 oz grated cheese
1 egg, beaten

Put the flour, salt, dry mustard and cayenne in a bowl, add the margarine and rub it in with the finger tips. Tip in the grated cheese and add the well beaten egg, mix thoroughly with a wooden spoon; if the mixture is too dry, add a little milk to make a nice firm dough. Tip out on to a floured board and press lightly with the palm of the hand until it's about 1″ thick. Cut into rounds with a cutter and place these on a greased baking sheet. Sprinkle each one with a little grated cheese and cook in a preheated oven (Gas 7, 425°F) for about 10 minutes when they should be a lovely golden brown.

Here's a way of using up those small potatoes that are left at the bottom of the bag.

Potato and raisin wine

2 lb old potatoes 1 lb pearl barley
1 gallon water 1 lb raisins
2 lb sugar (demerara is best) 1 tablespoon yeast

First scrub the potatoes clean and cut them into slices. Place them in a large saucepan and cover with the gallon of water, and cook until they are quite soft, but not mushy. Into your wine pan put the sugar, pearl barley and the finely chopped raisins, then strain the potatoes and pour the hot liquid over the contents of the wine pan. (Tip the potatoes away, as you have taken all the goodness you want from them.) Stir the wine and when it's cool, but not cold, sprinkle on the yeast. Cover with a thick cloth and leave to work for a week. Strain, and put the wine into a demijohn, fix the air lock and leave until all fermentation has stopped. Bottle off and cork lightly for the first week or so. This wine is better for keeping, but should be ready to drink at Christmas if made in March. Mind you, I don't throw *my* potatoes away, well, only to the hens, and they soon gobble them up.

APRIL

I think that this is the best time of the year, with all the cottage gardens bright with daffodils and forsythia. When I cycled to the shop today I thought the village green looked quite beautiful, all green and tidy it was. It's such a peaceful setting with the cottages all around, I suppose it's not altered much in the past two hundred years. But there's more to do this month than just think about the past, for this is the time for spring cleaning, and Mrs Doris Archer is nearly always the first to start. She and Mr Archer came into the shop yesterday to get all her cleaning materials. Dan was like a bear with a sore head, he was mumbling about 'no proper hot meals for days'.

'Don't you believe him, Martha,' Mrs Archer said, 'we won't do so bad.' I knew what she meant; during the next few days it would be stews and soups and milk puddings, all things that she could just put in the oven early in the morning and they would need little or no attention while she got on with her work – so I've included one or two of her special spring-cleaning recipes in this chapter.

Mind you, I'm always glad when spring-cleaning time comes round, it gives me a good excuse to turf out things that we haven't used for ages. And strange as it may seem, there's always two or three jumble sales in the village at this time of year, so I'm able to give a bit of stuff to each of them.

I think this recipe for potato and celery soup came from Nora Macaully. It uses up the small potatoes and any odd bits of tough celery.

Potato and celery soup

1 lb potatoes	1 bay leaf
1 onion	½ oz flour
A few stalks of celery	½ pint milk
½ oz dripping	Salt and pepper
1 pint water	1 dessertspoon chopped parsley

Peel and slice the potatoes and the onion, and chop the celery up quite small. Melt the dripping and fry the vegetables lightly for a few minutes. Tip them into a saucepan and add the water and bay leaf. Bring up to the boil and cook gently until the potatoes are cooked. Mash them with the fork against the side of the saucepan, without removing them. Mix the flour with the milk and add this to the soup. Cook for another 3 minutes, season and sprinkle on the parsley just before serving.

This is one of the meals Mrs Archer cooks during the spring-cleaning season but it makes a very tasty dinner any time I think.

Casseroled neck of mutton

2 lb best end neck of mutton
1 oz dripping
Salt and pepper to taste
½ lb onions

½ teaspoon mixed herbs
(dried)
1 small tomato
2 meat cubes
Stock or water

Cut the meat up into chop-like portions, put the dripping in the frying pan and fry the meat very lightly in the dripping. Lay the meat in the casserole adding the pepper and salt. Now fry the onions for a few minutes and then add them to the casserole too, but be very careful not to tip any of the fat from the frying pan in. Add the herbs, tomato, and crumbled meat cubes, and enough stock or water to cover all the ingredients. Place the lid on and cook slowly for 3 hours at Gas 3, 335°F.

If the meat is very fat, even after you have trimmed it, then it's a good idea to cook the casserole the day before it's needed. Then when the dish is cold you can take off the excess fat and just gently re-heat ready for dinner.

Beef casserole with dumplings

1 lb stewing beef
¼ lb kidney
1 tablespoon flour, salt and
    pepper
1 oz dripping

½ lb onions
A sprig of thyme
Stock or water
½ lb carrots, peeled and sliced

For the dumplings
½ lb self-raising flour
¼ lb suet
Pinch of salt

¼ teaspoon parsley
¼ teaspoon thyme
Water to mix to a soft dough

Cut the meat up into 1″ cubes. Place the flour, salt and pepper on a plate, dip each piece of meat in it, then fry it for a few minutes in the hot dripping. Tip the beef and kidney into the casserole and then fry the onions and put them on top of it. Any seasoned flour left on the plate should be tipped in as well, this will help to make the gravy nice and thick. Add the sprig of thyme (which you should take out before dishing up the meal). Fill the casserole up with stock or water and cook in a slowish oven (Gas 3, 335°F) for 3 hours, before adding the peeled sliced carrots, and continue cooking for a further ½ hour.

Mix all the dumpling ingredients together into little balls and drop into the casserole. Cook for another ½ hour.

Stuffed shoulder of lamb

Easter falls this month and I always think that spring lamb and rhubarb and date tart (see page 77 for the recipe) is nice for Easter Sunday dinner. Here's a way of making a shoulder, or even half a shoulder of lamb, go quite a long way.

	Stuffing
Shoulder of lamb	4 oz breadcrumbs
A little flour	2 teaspoons chopped mint
2 tablespoons suet or	1 egg
dripping	Salt and pepper
	1 small onion, chopped

Try and get your butcher to bone the joint for you, then there will be slits or pockets in the meat. Mix up all the stuffing ingredients together. Fill the pockets or slits with the stuffing, then roll the joint up quite loosely. Either tie it up or put several skewers in to keep the roll intact. Now dredge the joint with flour and put it in a meat tin. Dot several knobs of suet or dripping on the meat and cook in a hottish oven (Gas 6, 400°F) for about 1½ hours. Baste the meat two or three times during the cooking. This is very nice eaten hot at dinner time with Yorkshire pudding and really tasty when it's cold; we love it for Sunday supper with a bit of my home-made green tomato chutney (see page 183 for recipe).

Yorkshire pudding

It's funny how recipes differ, both Mrs Doris Archer and Mrs P. add a tablespoon of cold water to their batter, just before they cook it, and Norah says that she finds a tablespoon of cooking oil added just before cooking improves her Yorkshire pudding. We are very fond of it, so I serve it with lamb or pork as well as with traditional roast beef.

4 oz plain flour	1 egg
Good pinch salt	½ pint milk

Place the flour and salt in a basin, add unbeaten egg and a little of the milk. Stir with a fork and beat till smooth. Add the rest of the milk and beat until small bubbles appear on the top of the batter (like pancake batter). Yorkshire batter is best made an hour or two before it is needed. I always cook my Yorkshire pudding along with the meat, but it can be cooked separately by just pouring some of the hot dripping from the roasting pan into the baking tin and pouring the batter straight in. Cook first on a low shelf in oven (Gas 7, 425°F) for 15 minutes, then move to the top shelf and cook for a further 15 minutes, until risen and nice and brown.

But, if you wish to cook it in the same tin as the meat this is what you do. About half an hour before the meal is to be eaten, pour off almost all the fat from the meat tin, leaving the joint in. Surround the meat with the batter and cook in the centre of the oven for about half an hour. If you have a small metal meat rack, place the meat on this. While the batter is cooking all the juice from the meat drips on to the middle of the pudding – super!

Pat Archer's potato, cheese and ham pasty

Now this recipe young Pat Archer gave me, she said that it was used a lot in Wales. Miners' wives use it because it makes a nice tasty pasty, the sort of thing that they would pack up in their husbands' dinner boxes. I make it often for my Joby, and when young Neil lived with us he always enjoyed it ever so.

For the pastry
½ lb self-raising flour   1 egg
3 oz lard and margarine, mixed with a little water

For the filling
¼ lb fat ham   3 sage leaves
1 large onion   ¼ lb mashed potato
Pepper and salt   2 oz tasty cheese, grated

Make up the pastry, roll out and cut into 2 rounds. Line a greased sandwich tin with one of the pastry rounds. Cut ham into small pieces and lay on the pastry. Then add the finely sliced onion, pepper and salt. Now chop the sage leaves up very small, beat into the mashed potato and cover the onion and ham with it. Sprinkle the grated cheese on top. Put the other pastry round on the top, brush over with a little milk or egg and cook in a moderate oven (Gas 5, 380°F) for about an hour. This is lovely hot with chips or cold with salad.

I often casserole an oldish bird (one that's finished laying) but the same recipe can be used for quite a young chicken, only in the case of the young bird the cooking time would be about half that of an old one. Pluck and prepare it in the same way as you would the pheasant on page 25. But this is how you cook it.

Hen or chicken cooked in wine

Ingredients

1 hen or chicken	3 tomatoes
1 tablespoon flour, salt and pepper	½ pint white wine
2 oz butter	Sprig each of parsley, thyme and marjoram
1 large onion	2 chicken cubes

Cut the bird up into joints and take off the skin if the bird is old. Dip each joint into the seasoned flour then fry in the butter, browning the joints on both sides. Tip these into a casserole, then peel and chop the onion and fry that until soft and add this to the chicken along with any seasoned flour left on the plate. Now add two or three bottled or tinned tomatoes, but fresh ones could of course be used. Pour over about ½ pint white wine (elderflower is a good one to use, but I expect any white wine would do just as well). Tie up the sprigs of herbs into a little bunch and drop these into the casserole. Crumble over the chicken cubes. Place in a preheated oven (Gas 4, 355°F) for about 1¼ hours for young birds, 2½ for an older bird. Don't forget to take out the bunch of herbs before dishing up.

Young Pat Archer came rushing into the shop the other morning, 'Martha,' she said, 'could I have about a pound and a half of cheese please as quick as you can cut it, strong if you've got it. I don't know what came over me, I forgot to put cheese on my order and I had planned to make a potato and cheese pie for our dinner today. You see I'm helping a bit more on the farm just now, so the meals have to be pretty simple.' I knew the recipe she was talking about, its one of Mrs Doris Archer's, and it must be the easiest thing in the world to make and yet it's tasty and nourishing.

Mrs Doris Archer's potato and cheese pie

About 1 lb cooked cold
  mashed potato
½ lb grated cheese

Salt and pepper
A few knobs of butter

Simply mix the mashed potato and grated cheese together, add the pepper and salt, place in a pie dish, dot with a few small knobs of butter and bake in a fairly hot oven (Gas 5, 380°F) for about 15 minutes when it will be nicely browned on top.

Casseroled carrots

Mrs Archer's daughter, Christine Johnson and Dorothy Adamson, the vicar's wife, were chatting in the shop the other afternoon. Mrs Adamson was saying that the carrots were getting a bit old and she would be glad when the new ones were ready to pull, when Mrs Johnson ups and says, 'You cook old carrots in a casserole, you'll find they are super that way.' 'All you do,' she went on, 'is scrape your carrots, say a pound, and put them through the coarse cutter of your mincer. Then put them in a casserole with a little pepper and salt, add half a cup of water and four or five little knobs of butter. Put the lid on and cook in a slow oven for about an hour. You'll find the flavour is super, and after cooking for an hour they are just ready to serve. You see they don't need straining because all the water has been absorbed.'

So a few nights later I cooked some in a casserole for Joby and me, and they really were a lovely flavour. All that my Joby said was 'Umm, these carrots are good,' and that's great praise coming from him.

Potato casserole

1½ lb potatoes	Pinch of pepper
1½ oz butter	3 oz strong cheese, grated
1 teaspoon salt	Scant ½ pint boiling milk

Peel the potatoes and slice thinly. Rub the inside of a baking dish with a knob of the butter. Spread half the potatoes in the bottom of a baking dish. Divide over them half the salt, pepper, cheese and butter. Lay over them the rest of the potatoes and season them. Spread on the rest of the cheese and dot with the remaining butter. Pour on the boiling milk. Bring to a simmer on top of the stove and then put in a hot oven (Gas 7, 425°F) for 20–30 minutes until the potatoes are tender, milk has been absorbed and the top nicely browned.

I know Mrs Doris Archer is a great one for saving fuel and that when she has the oven on for such a long while she fills it up with as much food as she can, perhaps cooking both the neck of mutton and the beef casserole on the same day, then all she would have to do is to warm one of them up for the following day. As well as this there would be one or two milk puddings cooking at the same time. Here's her special spring-cleaning rice pudding:

Mrs Doris Archer's rice pudding

2 heaped tablespoons rice
1 tablespoon honey or
  golden syrup
1 pint milk

A knob of butter
Sprinkling of nutmeg
1 tablespoon thick cream

Wash the rice in cold water and drain well. Place it with the honey or syrup and milk into a baking dish. Add the knob of butter and sprinkle nutmeg on the top. Cook for 2 or 3 hours on the lower shelf at Gas 3, 335°F. Just before serving stir in a good tablespoon of thick cream.

If you have no stewed fruit to serve with the rice pudding, a spoonful of home-made jam makes a nice change.

Mary Pound tells me that she nearly always puts about two ounces of sultanas in her rice pudding. 'I got no time to stew fruit or anything fancy like that,' she told me, 'and them sultanas makes it a bit more nourishing and tasty for my Ken.'

Rhubarb and date tart

Walter Gabriel always brings me a bit of early forced rhubarb. He grows it, he says, just for the ladies of his choice as he calls Mrs Perkins, Mrs Doris Archer and myself, in that order. Mrs Perkins usually has hers quite a week before me, and I always know when Walter has taken hers, because she comes in to the shop and the first thing she asks for is a lemon, always puts a slice or two of lemon in her stewed rhubarb she does. But really it's to let me know that *she* has already had her rhubarb. She has never quite got over the fact that it was quite a strong job between me and Walter, before I met my Joby that was.

But we like a rhubarb and date tart, and you don't need to use any sugar because the dates provide the sweetness.

Shortcrust pastry
8 oz self-raising flour
4 oz margarine
1 oz lard
1 egg
Pinch of salt

Filling
3 or 4 sticks young rhubarb
½ lb chopped dates
The juice of 1 lemon
½ teaspoon powdered
  cinnamon

Make up your shortcrust pastry, adding a little water if necessary, but if you use a large egg it should be just about the right consistency. Roll out and line a greased sandwich tin with half of it. Simply wipe the rhubarb, there should be no need to peel it if it's nice and young. Cut it up into small pieces and lay it on the pastry, cover that with the chopped dates. Squeeze over the lemon juice and the cinnamon. Cover over with thinly rolled out pastry and press the whole tart down lightly with the hand. Make a few cuts across the pastry sort of criss-cross fashion. Bake in a hot oven (Gas 7, 425°F), for about ½ hour, when the pastry should be nice and golden.

Rhubarb sponge

And here's a quick, easy sponge pudding which could be cooking at the same time as the potato and cheese pie on page 74.

5 or 6 sticks rhubarb	3 oz sugar
2 tablespoons golden syrup	1 large egg
4 oz margarine	5 oz self-raising flour

Wipe the rhubarb, cut it into short pieces and stew gently for a few minutes with the syrup. Then place in a pie dish. Beat up the margarine and sugar together, then add the egg – well beaten – and lastly the flour. You may need a few spots of milk to make a nice thick mixture. Spread this over the part cooked rhubarb and place in a moderate oven (Gas 5, 380°F) for about ½ hour. Serve hot with cream or custard.

Mrs Blossom's Easter biscuits

Mrs Blossom came in to see me the other day just before Easter. 'I've brought you a little present,' she said. Well, I was quite overwhelmed when she handed me a little parcel.

'Can I open it now?' I asked.

''Course you can, it's nothing really, just something that I thought you and your husband might like to eat over the holiday.' She had baked some Easter biscuits, and had been round the village taking a few to each of her friends. I did think that it was a nice thought. 'And I've written out the recipe,' she added, 'I know how keen you are about trying out different things.'

Well I tried them and they were very nice. A couple of weeks after Mrs Blossom had given me them, it was our W.I. meeting and it was my turn, along with Jill Archer, to do the refreshments. So I made a great batch of these Easter biscuits, enough for every member to have one each, and they did enjoy them, while Jill had made some feather-iced biscuits and they were very popular too.

3 oz margarine	Pinch of salt
3 oz caster sugar	$\frac{1}{4}$ teaspoon mixed pudding
1 egg yolk	spice
1 oz mixed peel	6 oz plain flour
1 oz currants	A little milk

Cream the fat and the sugar together, then beat in the egg yolk. Now add the finely chopped peel, currants, salt and spice and lastly fold in the flour. Mix to a nice soft dough, with a few drops of milk if necessary. Roll out lightly on a floured board to about $\frac{1}{8}"$ thick, cut into rounds and prick each biscuit several times. Place on a greased baking sheet and cook in a fairly hot oven (Gas 6, 400°F) for about 20 minutes, until they are a nice light creamy colour. Remove from the baking sheet and cool the biscuits on a cake tray.

Jill Archer's feather-iced biscuits

Biscuit mix	*Glacé icing*
3 oz margarine or butter	4 oz icing sugar, sieved
3 oz sugar	$1\frac{1}{2}$ tablespoons warm water
1 egg	Squeeze lemon juice
Pinch of salt	A little cocoa or drinking
6 oz plain flour	chocolate to make the main
Vanilla essence	part of the icing a creamy
Milk and water to mix	colour

Cream the fat and sugar together and then add the egg. Add the salt and flour and lastly a few drops of vanilla essence, and mix it all up to make a nice soft dough with a little of the milk and water. Roll out to about $\frac{1}{8}''$ thick. Cut into any fancy shapes that you may have and prick each biscuit with a fork. Place on a baking tray (or sheet as I sometimes call it) and cook for about 18 minutes in a moderate oven (Gas 4, 355°F). Remove from the baking sheet and allow the biscuits to get quite cold.

To make the icing, put the sieved icing sugar into a saucepan, along with the water, lemon juice and colouring. Heat up slowly stirring all the while. Don't let the mixture get hot, but just warm. Now ice the biscuits, but just dropping a little of the mixture on each. Make sure to leave a bit of the icing in the pan, and keep it warm, now stir in a little cocoa or drinking chocolate to this small amount of icing. Put it into your icing bag with a very fine nozzle on and quickly draw lines across the biscuits, then draw a skewer up and down at right angles to the lines and this will make a nice feathered effect.

It was Betty Tucker, wife of Mike, who gave me this simple little recipe for making rhubarb and mint jelly; it's beautiful with a nice bit of young lamb and makes quite a change from mint sauce.

Rhubarb and mint jelly

Rhubarb	Sugar	Fresh mint

Try and use nice pinky red rhubarb for this, I think colour in any cooking is most important.

Wipe the rhubarb but don't peel it and cut it into small pieces. Place in a saucepan along with a cup of water and cook until the fruit is soft. Strain through a fine sieve until you have got all the juice out. Measure the juice carefully and put into a preserving pan or saucepan and add a pound of sugar to each pint of juice. Pick some fresh mint and tie it into a bundle and boil this up with the juice and sugar for about 20 minutes. Test to see if the jelly is set by putting a little on a saucer, leave a moment to get cold then push your finger across the jam; if a skin has formed the jelly will set. Take out the bundle of mint and pour the jelly into small dry pots. Tie down when it's cool.

Parsley wine

I like to make two lots of parsley wine each year, one in April, when, if we've had a mildish winter the parsley will have survived and grown thick and strong and quite dark looking in colour. Then I make another lot about August time with a younger, greener parsley. And, of course, the two wines taste very different. But it certainly is both mine and Joby's favourite.

1 lb parsley picked free from stalks	2 oranges
	2 lemons
1 gallon water	4 lb sugar
1 piece root ginger, (about as big as a walnut)	½ oz yeast

Put your parsley into your wine crock and pour the gallon of boiling water over it. Cover and let it stand for two days.

Now strain and boil up the liquor for 20 minutes with the root ginger, and the grated rinds of the oranges and lemons. Then pour the hot liquor on to the sugar and the juice from the fruit. When cool, but not quite cold, sprinkle on the yeast. Cover with a thick cloth and leave for 4–5 days. Strain once more and pour into a demijohn, fix the air lock and leave until all the working has stopped. Then bottle off. The wine will be ready to drink in 6 months – but of course will improve if you can manage to leave it longer.

Down the lane towards our cottage the hedges are bowing down with the weight of the May blossom. I don't think I have ever seen it so thick and lovely as it is this year. And it's a pleasure to cycle through the village these days for the scent from the flower gardens is quite heady and strong, everywhere is ablaze with tulips, forget-me-nots and gilly flowers. I stopped and picked a lovely bunch of cowslips this morning, I don't think there is anything that smells as sweet as cowslips. Mind you, there are plenty growing along the grass verges and in the fields around; if they were scarce then I'd leave 'um be. Well, the weather has certainly turned a bit warmer, but summer's not here yet, although I have heard the old cuckoo singing over Lakey Hill way. It's funny, every spring country folk long to hear the cuckoos' calling, yet before you know where you are they are flying back to Africa, or wherever they come from.

Mrs Blossom came in quite early this morning, she's house-keeper for Mr Lucas who rents the dower house, the one that Ralph and Lilian Bellamy own. 'Course we never see Mr Lucas and Mrs Blossom says he's got some very queer eating habits, he told her he wanted some lettuce and spring onion soup. 'Coo,' I told her, 'I can't imagine my Joby eating lettuce and onion soup.'

Still, there's no accounting for taste is there, and if he wants lettuce soup then Mrs Blossom will have to cook it for him. So I asked her how she made it.

Mrs Blossom's lettuce and onion soup

'Well,' she said, 'you need a lettuce and about a dozen spring onions, a pint of milk, a knob of dripping and a tablespoon of cornflour. Ah that's what I came in for,' she went on, 'some plain cornflour. Then you want salt and pepper of course and a sprinkling of nutmeg, a teaspoon of sugar and a few parsley leaves and some crusts of bread. It's quite simple to make really,' she said, 'you just wash the lettuce and shred it up, then peel the onions and chop them up fine and fry both the lettuce and onion for about five minutes. Next you add the milk and simmer for about 10 minutes. Then mix the cornflour with a cup of cold water and tip that into the soup and boil up again. Sprinkle on the nutmeg, sugar, salt and pepper. While all this is going on you cut some slices of bread and cut it up again to about inch strips and put them on a tray in a warm oven for about 20 minutes to crisp up. Lay the crisp bread in a soup tureen, sprinkle finely cut parsley leaves over, then pour over the hot soup and serve at once. Oh yes,' she said, 'Mr Lucas really likes his spring soup.'

I was taught never to waste bread. And when you come to think of the work that goes into producing it, I mean from the time of planting the corn seed right up until you get a loaf on your tea table, none of us should ever waste any. Apart from the dozens of ways that you can use up stale bread in cooking, you can easily make your own breadcrumbs for frying food in, like the birds' nests that Sid Perks concocted. (See the recipe on page 89). All you need to do is just put any crusts or pieces of stale bread on a baking tray. Place them in a warm oven until they are nice and crisp and brown, then crush them very finely with a rolling pin or milk bottle. Store in a screwtop jar.

Here's another way of using up breadcrumbs, and any bits of fat bacon that you might have. You can use minced beef or lamb and I have heard Mrs Phil say that she has even used raw chicken to make it. It's a very handy thing to have in the larder, a meat and bread roll, because you can fill sandwiches with it, or have it cut thick and serve it with pickles and chutney or salads. It's even lovely eaten hot with mashed potatoes and any other available vegetables. You see it's full of goodness and very tasty, and so easy to make.

Meat and bread roll

½ lb fresh minced meat	Salt and pepper
¼ lb fat bacon pieces (cut very small)	1 teaspoon chopped parsley
	1 teaspoon chopped thyme
½ lb breadcrumbs	2 eggs, beaten

Simply mix all the ingredients together, binding it quite firmly with the beaten eggs, and place the mixture in a greased loaf or bread tin. Bake in a warmish oven (Gas 4, 355°F) for about 1½ hours.

Mrs Laura Archer is not too interested in cooking. I suppose this was because for years she didn't have to bother about it, because Fairley, her help and chauffeur did most of the cooking. But sometimes, when she's not worrying about council business, or church affairs, she will talk about the old days back in New Zealand. It was she who gave me this idea as how to cook lamb cutlets with mint; it makes a really nice change too.

Mrs Laura Archer's grilled lamb cutlets with mint

4 lamb cutlets
1 good tablespoon very finely chopped mint

1 oz butter
Black pepper and a little salt
Squeeze of lemon juice

Chop the mint very finely then add the butter and mix to a paste. Season with black pepper, a little salt and the squeeze of lemon juice. Lightly score the cutlets on both sides and coat with the mint butter and leave for an hour. Light the grill at top heat and cook the cutlets for about 10 minutes, turning them twice during the cooking time. If there is room on the grill cook some halved tomatoes at the same time. Pour off any butter liquid left in the grill pan onto the cutlets and tomatoes. Serve hot. Lovely with chips and peas.

Lamb leftovers

Here is a quick little tip to use up any leftover lamb from the Sunday joint. Serve this with spring cabbage and potatoes mashed with a little warm milk and butter.

Place slices of cold roast lamb in a baking tin, then mix together:

2 tablespoons margarine
$\frac{3}{4}$ tablespoon vinegar
$\frac{1}{4}$ teaspoon dry mustard

Salt and pepper
1 tablespoon redcurrant jelly

Warm the mixture very gently and pour over the lamb. Serve at once.

Now this next recipe is certainly in my line. Polly told me how to cook these birds' nests, but she said that it was really one of Sid's concoctions. He does have a little go at cooking now and then though not all of his culinary efforts are as good as this. But this one makes a nice supper snack.

Sid and Polly's birds' nests

2 hard boiled eggs	Egg and breadcrumbs
2 tablespoons cold mashed potato	Fat for frying
	Buttered toast
½ teaspoon curry powder	

Hard boil the eggs, one for each person. Mash up the potato with the curry powder and cover the eggs with it, shaping with the hands. Now roll them in the egg and breadcrumbs, and fry in hot fat until golden brown. Cut the covered eggs in half and serve on buttered toast.

Well, young Jennifer Aldridge came in to the shop last Tuesday. She's a lovely girl and I'm so glad that she's found herself a nice husband. He's ever such a pleasant young man and a very good farmer by all accounts.

'I've run out of Worcester sauce, Martha,' she said, 'please say that you have some in stock?'

I said, 'Yes, of course I have, there's aren't many things

you come in for that I can't supply you with, now is there?' She agreed that I do very well for a village shop. 'What are you making special that you must have Worcester sauce for?' I enquired. `

'Fish ramekins, Martha, I discovered ages ago that they are one of Brian's favourite dishes, so tonight that's what I'm going to cook for him.'

I had to admit that ramekins were something that I had never tried, and I didn't think they was quite up my street.

'You should try everything once, Martha, look I'll scribble the recipe down and one of these fine days I shall come in you'll tell me that you've tried it and that you've converted Joby into eating it.' Well I must admit I still haven't cooked it, but I just might one day.

Jennifer Aldridge's fish ramekins

1 lb cold cooked fish	*White sauce*
A little milk	1 oz butter
1½ cups white sauce	1 oz plain flour
2 oz grated cheese	½ pint milk
2 teaspoons Worcester sauce	Salt and pepper
Salt and pepper to taste	
1 tablespoon breadcrumbs	

First make up the white sauce by melting the butter in a pan, stir in the flour, then add the milk, stirring all the time. Boil for 5 minutes, then season to taste.

Now flake the fish into a basin, add a little milk and the made up white sauce, 1½ oz of the grated cheese and Worcester sauce. Season to taste and mix well. Put into buttered ramekin dishes, sprinkle with the breadcrumbs and a little more grated cheese. Bake in a moderate oven (Gas 4, 355°F), top shelf, for about 20 minutes. Serve at once.

What in the world I wonder are ramekin dishes like!

For the next couple of months there will be rhubarb aplenty and it's a good idea to use it up while it's nice and young and tender. This recipe for rhubarb soufflé makes a very special treat. And it is one of Doris Archer's favourites.

Mrs Doris Archer's rhubarb soufflé

8 sticks young rhubarb
1 breakfast cup of water
3 oz sugar
1 heaped teaspoon of plain
    cornflour
A few drops vanilla essence

3 eggs, separated
3 oz caster sugar
½ pint milk
The grated rind and
    juice of half a lemon

Wipe the rhubarb, but don't peel it, then cut it up into about 1″ pieces. Boil the water and sugar together, then add the rhubarb and simmer until it's cooked, but still in pieces and *not* mushy. Take the rhubarb out, drain it (keeping the juice), and lay in a fair-sized pie or baking dish. Now blend the cornflour with a little water to make a paste, tip in the rhubarb juice and simmer in a saucepan until the mixture becomes clear and syrupy. Add the few drops of vanilla essence. Pour this over the rhubarb that is in the baking dish, and put on one side to cool. Now separate the eggs. Beat up the yolks and add the caster sugar. Stir until the mixture is nice and creamy. Heat the milk (don't let it boil) and pour it over the egg and sugar mixture. Put this in a basin and stand the basin over a saucepan of boiling water to cook, stirring all the time until it thickens, making it into egg custard. Take off the heat, set this aside to cool and then add the lemon juice and grated rind. Now beat up the egg whites very stiffly and gradually add them to the now cool custard. Pour this mixture over the rhubarb and syrup. Bake for ¾ hour (Gas 4, 355°F) on the middle shelf. Serve at once.

The Archers' beestings pudding

Beestings, as most country folk know, is the milk that a cow gives after she has just had a calf. Some people don't use the very first milk as it is a very deep colour, but after the first milking the farmer's wife usually makes the most of this very rich milk. It can be used to make a lovely custard, but of course you don't need to use eggs with it. Other sorts of puddings can be made with it too and soft cheese can be made from beestings as well. But as we are not all able to get hold of this very rich milk I will just give one or two of the most popular recipes. The first is one that most of the ladies in the Archer family have made at one time or another, them being farmers' wives. Young Pat Archer is especially keen on using beestings.

And remember, one breakfast cup of beestings is equal to two eggs in a Yorkshire pudding.

1½ pints beestings milk	1 oz brown sugar
1 oz cornflour	2 oz currants or saltanas

Grease a good sized pie dish. Mix together the beestings milk and cornflour until smooth. Into the pie dish put the brown sugar, and currants or sultanas, stir in the milk and cornflour and bake in a slowish oven (Gas 3, 335°F) until golden brown and set. This will take about ½ – ¾ hour.

Super beestings custard

1 pint beestings   Pinch of salt
2 tablespoons sugar   Sprinkling of nutmeg

Stir into the pint of beestings the sugar and salt. Put into a
pie dish and sprinkle on the nutmeg to taste. Bake in a
coolish oven (Gas 3, 335°F) for about $\frac{1}{2}$ – $\frac{3}{4}$ hour until set like
an egg custard.

Chocolate and biscuit crunch

This is an easy little recipe, and just the thing for clearing up
those odds and ends of biscuits you might have in the
bottom of the biscuit tin.

4 oz cooking chocolate   6 oz broken biscuits
4 oz margarine or butter   Few drops vanilla
1 egg   essence

First melt the chocolate and margarine in separate basins
over hot water. Now beat up the egg and add the melted
margarine or butter and chocolate. Crumble the biscuits just
by squeezing them in your hand, then stir them into the
chocolate and margarine mixture, then add the essence and
stir again. Put into a greased flat tin, press down and leave
for 2 hours to cool in the bottom of the fridge. You can vary
this by adding a few chopped nuts or cherries, or raisins.

When people come into the shop and buy concentrated mint sauce, it makes me wonder why on earth they don't make a good stock of it when there's plenty of fresh mint about in the gardens. I always make some at this time of the year, then come the wintertime use my own concentrated sort. You see the mint plants usually die down in the autumn, only to come up as thick as mustard and cress again each springtime. Well here's how you make it.

Home-made concentrated mint sauce

1 breakfast cup finely chopped mint leaves	½ pint vinegar 6 oz sugar

Put the vinegar and sugar in a saucepan and bring it up to the boil. Take off the heat and add the chopped mint. Stir with a wooden spoon to mix it up well and when the mixture is cold put it into a screw topped jar – a preserving jar will do as long as you don't fill it right up, you don't want the vinegar to touch the tin top. All you do when you want to serve mint sauce with lamb, is to take out about a dessert-spoonful, mix this with a little fresh vinegar to the right consistency and it's ready for use. This will keep for a year.

Here's another way of using up fresh mint; this is lovely with lamb, specially cold lamb, and needs no cooking.

Mint chutney

4 tablespoons chopped mint
½ large cup chopped raisins
1 tablespoon brown sugar
  (soft, not demerara)

2 tablespoons tomato
  ketchup or sauce
A squeeze of lemon juice
Salt to taste

Pick the leaves off the stems and rinse them under the tap, then chop them up finely. Now chop the raisins too and mix them with the mint. Now add the soft brown sugar, the tomato ketchup and a squeeze of lemon juice. Sprinkle on the salt (you will only need about a couple of pinches). Stir the chutney with a wooden spoon until all the ingredients are well mixed. Put into jam-jars and tie down with grease-proof or brown paper. This is ready to use straight away but will keep well for 8 or 9 months if it's stored in a dry larder.

Rhubarb wine

If you make this wine in May or early June, it will be just right to drink at Christmas time.

4 lb rhubarb (pink if possible
  to make a nice pinky wine)
1 gallon water
4 lb sugar

2 lemons
½ oz root ginger
½ oz yeast

Wipe the sticks of rhubarb clean but do not peel. Cut up into pieces about 2″ long, place in a crock and crush. Pour on the gallon of cold water, cover with a thick cloth and leave for 6 days. Skim off scum which will have formed on the top of the liquor and strain. Now add the sugar, the juice and rind of the lemons and the root ginger. Stir well and place the yeast on the top of the wine and let this stand for another 6 days. Strain, put into a demijohn, fix the airlock and leave until fermentation has ceased. Then bottle the wine, only corking lightly at first.

Mary Pound's elderflower champagne

This is the simplest thing to make – mind you it's not a wine, but just a very nice summer drink. Mary reckons that she and Ken drink quarts of it during the summertime, you see it's a good thirst quencher, and quite cheap to make too. Be careful though to pick the flowers when they're just out and not falling otherwise it would make the champagne bitter.

2 heads of elderflowers	2 tablespoons white wine
1 lemon	vinegar
1½ lb white sugar	1 gallon of cold water

Pick the heads when in full bloom. Take off any green stems, however small. Put the blossoms into a bowl, sprinkle over the juice from the lemon, grate the rind and add this along with the sugar and vinegar. Add the cold water and leave for 24 hours. Strain into bottles and cork firmly and lay the bottles on their sides. Don't disturb for 2 weeks, when the champagne should be sparkling and ready to drink. Don't try and keep this drink as you would wine, but it will keep easily for 2–3 months.

Walter Gabriel's granny's elderflower wine

While we are thinking about elderflowers I would like you to try making wine the way that Walter Gabriel's granny made it, or so he says. Wherever the recipe came from it's a good one and very easy to follow. I make gallons of it, it seems such a pity not to make the most of some of those lovely blossoms from the hedgerows.

3 pints elderflowers measured   3 lb sugar
   in a pint cup, jug or basin)   2 oranges
1 gallon cold water   2 lemons
1 small piece root ginger   ½ oz yeast

Pick the flowers on a sunny day, they must not be too full out and the petals falling. Pick all the green stalks from the elderflowers, place them in a saucepan and cover them with the water; add the root ginger bring to the boil, and simmer for 15 minutes. Add the sugar and the rind of the lemons and oranges. Bring up to boil again and simmer for further 15 minutes. Strain into a pan or plastic bucket and add the juice from the lemons and oranges. While still warm (but not too hot) sprinkle on the yeast. Cover with a cloth and leave for about a week. Strain again, pour into a demijon, fix airlock and leave in the jar until all fermentation has stopped. Bottle off and leave at least 6 months before drinking.

JUNE

There's nothing so lovely as the warm light nights that we have in June. It's so nice to be able to sit outside in the garden at 10 o'clock in the evenings in the dimpsy light, eating your supper and watching the swifts and swallows darting about in the sky, with night air full of the scent from the roses and lilies. I think that most flowers smell stronger in the evenings when the dew is on them. The horsechestnut trees are out in full blossom just now, but we always call them Whitsuntide candles in Ambridge; when you come to think of it that's what they look like too, giant candles in great green candlesticks. Joby and me love this time of the year, well I think most folk do, specially country folk.

It's a busy time for the housewife though. There's the soft fruit to pick and jams and jelly to be made – gooseberry and strawberry, with the early raspberries and redcurrants ripening by the end of the month; it takes me all my time to keep the blackbirds off the strawberries. I noticed that Mrs Jill Archer has got a lovely big fruit cage in her garden with all her soft fruits growing in it. I shall have to see if my Joby can't fix me up with something like that, for I swear those blessed birds eat a darned sight more of our fruit than we do.

In Joby's mum's cookbook there are several ways to cook pig's liver. I expect they kept their own pigs in those days, most country folk did anyway. This is one meal that we are very fond of, it includes pig's liver and home-cured streaky bacon, not that we can always get either nowadays, but liver and bacon bought from any butcher or supermarket would do.

Liver and bacon
(as Joby's mum cooked it)

2 good sized onions	Salt and pepper
1 large cooking apple	1 teaspoon each of
1 lb pigs liver	chopped parsley and
½ lb streaky rashers	marjoram
6 oz breadcrumbs	Water

Peel the onions and apple and slice them thinly. Cut up the rashers into small pieces and the liver in thin slices. Into a nice big casserole put a layer of liver, followed by a layer of bacon, then a good sprinkling of breadcrumbs, apples and onions, followed by about half the herbs. Repeat these layers until you have used up all the ingredients, making sure that the last thing is breadcrumbs. Now fill the casserole with water so that it just covers the breadcrumbs. Put the lid on and cook for about 2 hours in a moderate oven (Gas 4, 355°F). Remove the lid and cook for a further ¼ hour.

Stuffed pig's heart

1 or 2 pig's hearts	Potatoes for baking with the
Dripping for baking	hearts

For the stuffing

3 oz breadcrumbs	1 small egg
1 good sized onion, chopped	1 oz dripping
1 heaped teaspoon chopped sage leaves	Salt and pepper

This is another recipe I found in the old cookbook. You can eat it hot with baked potatoes or cold cut up in slices and served with salad, either way it's very tasty.

Wash the hearts, cut out the pipes with kitchen scissors and remove any blood. Make up the stuffing by mixing the breadcrumbs, the chopped onion and the sage leaves together. Add the egg and the dripping and pepper and salt to taste. Stuff the hearts with this mixture, and sew up the tops with strong thread, to keep the stuffing in. Place in a baking tin, cover the hearts with dripping, surround them with halves of potatoes, and cook in a moderate oven (Gas 4, 355°F) for the first hour. Then turn the heat up to Gas 6, 400°F for ½ hour to crisp up the potatoes.

Barbara Drury's gammon pie

Mrs Drury the policeman's wife don't usually have a lot to say when she comes into the shop. Well, she's quite chatty to me if we are on our own, but as soon as anybody else comes in she shuts up like a clam. When I say chatty, I don't mean she has a laugh and a joke like Nora or Polly do when they come in, no, it's just talking about the weather and the high price of food, and now and then what she's going to get for her husband's dinner. Mind you, she's another housewife who never knows what time her husband's coming home.

But the other day she was quite cheerful and she told me that she was going to cook Colin's favourite meal, gammon pie. That was, if I had got some nice thick gammon rashers that she could buy. Well thankfully I'd just had a delivery of bacon so she was in luck. So she told me how she cooked it and since then I've passed the recipe on to Peggy and Mrs Laura Archer and they both said that it was the sort of meal that a person living on their own could make easily. Still there's nothing to stop the biggest family using the recipe as long as the amounts are increased.

- 1 gammon rasher for each person
- 1 medium sized cooking apple for each person
- 1 good sized potato for each person
- A little dripping
- Salt and pepper to taste

Have the bacon cut about ¾″ thick. Cut off the rind and fry the bacon lightly on both sides, then cut into pieces and place at the bottom of a pie dish. Peel the apples and cut into slices and lay over the bacon. Then peel the potato and slice that nice and thick and place over the apples. Season with pepper and salt. Cover the pie dish and cook for about an hour in a warm oven (Gas 3, 335°F). Take off the cover, dot with a few knobs of dripping and cook for another 20 minutes to crisp up the potatoes.

Cheesey chicken

1 chicken	1 egg
1 tablespoon flour	3 oz grated cheese
Salt and pepper	2 oz breadcrumbs

Cook the chicken by placing it in a large saucepan, cover with cold water, bring to the boil and then simmer for about an hour till the chicken is cooked. Take it out of the water and leave to cool and then cut the bird up into joints. Put the flour, salt and pepper on a plate and dip each chicken joint in it. Now beat up the egg and dip each joint in this. Have ready the grated cheese and breadcrumbs well mixed and dip each chicken piece in this, coating all over. Get your grill good and hot and cook the joints on both sides for a few minutes until golden brown. Place them on a fireproof dish and slip into a warm oven for about 20 minutes.

Polly came rushing into the shop this morning, so excited she was too. Sid had taken her out for a meal the night before, all unexpected like. They went up to Grey Gables and had dinner by candlelight. 'Oh Martha,' she cried, 'it was so lovely and quite romantic really, my Sid don't half know how to treat a gel when he wants to. I did enjoy the meal and being waited on,' she chatted on. 'We had sole meunière for the fish course, and I liked it so much I asked the waiter how it was cooked. I suppose it was a bit of a cheek really, but

I'd never had sole that tasted like that did. Anyhow when he brought the main course in he handed me this slip of paper with the recipe on. Not that I shall ever cook it like that, I don't suppose, but it's nice to have it all the same. Here, you can copy it out if you like, Martha,' she went on handing me the slip of paper, 'then you can try it out on your Joby sometime.'

Well, I scribbled it out quickly, but when I realised that it had to be served with slices of orange, I knew for sure my Joby wouldn't like that, remembering what he said when I served up slices of lemon on his pork chops! Anyhow, here's the recipe:

Sole meunière

1 sole	1 orange
1 tablespoon flour	1 tablespoon sherry
Salt and pepper	1 teaspoon vinegar
2 oz butter	

First skin the sole, wash it under the tap for a few minutes and then dry with a tea towel. Put the flour, salt and pepper on a plate and dip the fish in it, coating both sides. Into your frying pan put the 2 oz butter and fry the sole lightly on both sides, then take out the fish and put it into a flattish dish. Pour off the butter and put it on one side. Peel the orange and slice it thinly and put it in your frying pan along with the tablespoon of sherry, half the butter and the teaspoon of vinegar and just bring up nearly to boiling point. Now lift out the orange slices and lay them across the fish. Mix the seasoned flour (which was left on the plate after coating the fish) and the butter that was left over after cooking it with the sherry and vinegar, bring it up to the boil, stirring all the while, to make a nice sauce. Pour this round the fish and serve with cress or watercress.

Of course June is the month for asparagus. We don't grow any but Mrs Blossom says that there's quite a big bed of it up at the Manor gardens. I expect Mr Bellamy had that planted when he lived there. Mrs Blossom was telling me the other day that Mr Lucas, who she works for, loves asparagus and he has it cooked all sorts of ways. He likes soup made from it, flans and omelettes. He's specially fond of omelettes and will eat one at any meal of the day when it's in season. Yesterday she told me how it's made.

Mrs Blossom's asparagus omelette

'It's ever so simple to cook,' she said, 'you just take about six big heads of it, cut off the green stem and put that on one side – that'll do for the soup making. Then you chop up the heads into thin slices, add salt and pepper to taste, put them in a saucepan along with a tablespoon of milk and cook for about five or six minutes, until all the milk has been absorbed. Now beat up three eggs, melt a little butter in your omelette pan, and when it's hot pour in half of the beaten eggs, cook for about half a minute, then add the asparagus and the remainder of the eggs. Just cook until it sets and fold it up. Serve the omelette at once, either with a sprinkling of chopped parsley or watercress on the top. Oh yes,' she went on, 'Mr Lucas really enjoys that.'

Then I got to thinking that the only time I ever tasted asparagus was years and years ago when I was in service. Lily

Flack the kitchen maid and me just stared at one another, neither of us knowing what to do with the little green bundle of stuff that was on our plates. Then the cook said to us, 'it's for eating, not for staring at, this is how you eat it,' she said, picking up the green stalks in her fingers and it just seemed to slip down her throat. But I can't say that I enjoyed eating it.

Our W.I. garden party was held earlier this month, in Carol Tregorran's garden. A beautiful evening it was, nice and warm and sunny. The entertainment was just right too, a party of school children from Borchester (which included some of the children from Ambridge), gave a lovely display of country dancing. That took me back a bit I can tell you, to when I used to do the same dances at our summer school treats. The refreshments, as usual, were super. They had been made by Mrs Phil Archer and her strawberry tarts were out of this world. She said she had been making them all that afternoon, and I don't doubt it, for I believe I ate at least four of them. Well, they kept on bringing them round so we kept on eating them. And the strawberries came from the gardens at Brookfield which made them all the more enjoyable. Before I left for home I made a point of telling Mrs Archer how much I had enjoyed the refreshments. 'Ah, Martha,' she said, laughing, 'I know you, you want the recipe for them don't you?' Well, I had to admit that I would love to try and make some, they would be fine for Sunday tea, or for when young Neil comes over. A few days later she came into the shop for her groceries and handed me a nicely typed out recipe. 'I got Shula to do it for you Martha, she types so quickly, and makes a better job of it than I can with my one finger effort.'

Then the very next day Betty Tucker came in with a lovely punnet of strawberries. 'Here you are Martha,' she said, 'a present for a good gal.' Well I thought that was ever so nice of her, because I think they have a bit of a struggle to make ends meet. She and her husband work ever so hard. So the next day I had a go at making some of Jill's strawberry tarts and they turned out fine. You could have them for tea, made singly, or make a big one in a sandwich tin and then it would do for Sunday pudding.

Jill Archer's strawberry tarts

For the pastry
8 oz plain flour
5 oz butter
1 oz sugar
Pinch of salt
A little water

For the filling and topping
2 teaspoons arrowroot
1 cup water
2 tablespoons sugar
A few spots strawberry
 flavouring
A few spots red colouring
Double cream for topping

Make up the pastry by rubbing the butter into the flour until it looks like breadcrumbs, then add the sugar, salt and a little water to make a nice workable dough. Roll out quite thinly and cut into small rounds (as for mince pies). Grease a patty tin and line with pastry rounds and bake them. To make sure the little tarts keep their shape you can fill them with small pieces of bread, or haricot beans, (these can be used over and over again). Bake in a fairly hot oven (Gas 6, 400°F) for about 20 minutes. Take out the bread (or beans) and leave the pastry cases to cool while you make up the filling.

Mix up the arrowroot with a cup of water, add the sugar, the flavouring and colouring, put into a small saucepan and bring to the boil; continue boiling until the mixture is clear. Leave to cool until it is *just about to set* but not cold.

Place a good big firm ripe strawberry in the centre of each pastry case and then very gently pour over a little of the strawberry glaze, covering the fruit. Now whip up some double cream. Put a large piping nozzle into your forcing bag and put the whipped cream into it. When the glaze seems set just pipe a small circle round the edge of the tartlet. Mrs Jill told me that the tartlets can also be filled with tinned cherries, making the glaze with the juice from the tin, and of course the arrowroot.

Summer pudding

I always think that summer is really here when I'm able to make a summer pudding. This again is a very old recipe and one that Doris Archer first passed on to me. And although this recipe says 'use redcurrants and raspberries' I have found that it can be made with a mixture of red and black-currants, strawberries and a few ripe gooseberries, and some people even make it with rhubarb. Then later in the year you can make a 'late' summer pudding with blackberries. But here is the original way that Mrs Doris Archer makes it, and it's super.

½ lb redcurrants 4 oz sugar
½ lb raspberries 4–5 slices of bread
2 tablespoons water

Put the fruit, water and sugar into a saucepan and stew very gently for a few minutes until it's soft. Grease a 1 lb pudding basin. Now cut about 4 or 5 slices of bread (not too thick), remove the crusts and lightly butter them. Line the basin with the slices of bread, butter side to the basin. Now pour the hot cooked fruit into the basin and put a 'lid' of bread on top of the fruit. Place a saucer on the top and a weight on the saucer so that it presses the pudding down firm. Don't worry if some juice runs out at this point. (It's a good plan to make this summer pudding overnight, keeping it in the fridge or a cool place until dinnertime.) When you are ready to serve the pudding tip it out into a dish when you will find that all the lovely colour from the fruit has soaked into the bread and the pudding will be completely whole. Lovely served with cream, ice cream or cold custard.

Dorothy Adamson's raspberry delight

Here's another pudding that needs no cooking, and that's what we want during the summer-time, easier meals, so that we can enjoy the nice weather and do a bit of gardening too.

It was the vicar's wife, Dorothy Adamson, who told me how to make this lovely light pudding when she came in the other day for some gelatine and, me being a bit nosey, I asked her what she was going to use it for.

'Raspberry Delight, Martha,' she said. 'It was one of the parishioners in my husband's last parish who gave the recipe to me. Funny,' she went on, 'it must be one of those "county" things because I've told a few of my friends in the village about it and none of them seems to have heard of it before. I find it very useful,' said said, 'especially on Sundays, I can whip it up before we go to church and it's just ready for lunch.'

1 cupful raspberries	2 cups water
1½ cups granulated sugar	Juice of 1 lemon
2 level tablespoons gelatine	3 egg whites

First mash the raspberries with 1 cup of sugar. Now cover the gelatine with a little water and leave for 5 minutes. Bring the rest of the water to boil and stir in the softened gelatine and remaining ½ cup of sugar. When the gelatine has dissolved add the lemon juice and raspberries. Leave the mixture to cool but *not* set. Now beat the whites of the eggs until stiff and add them to the mixture. Beat all together until really smooth. Put into individual glasses and chill. Serve with cream.

Whitsuntide pie

When I was a youngster my mother always made a 'Whitsuntide pie' which was really just an ordinary gooseberry pie that we had on Whitsunday for our pudding. And I have followed up that tradition, for we have plenty of gooseberry bushes in our garden. Young Neil couldn't get over the fact that country folk have special things to eat at certain times during the year, he said the only time that he and his family had anything special was at Christmas. Anyhow I think it's rather nice to keep up some of the old customs, so here's my mother's recipe.

Filling

1½ lb gooseberries (topped and tailed)	½ teaspoon cinnamon
	¼ teaspoon nutmeg
4 oz sugar (2 oz more if you have a sweet tooth)	1 cup water

Shortcrust pastry

8 oz self-raising flour	1 oz lard
4 oz margarine	1 small egg

Put all the filling ingredients into a saucepan and cook gently until the fruit is almost cooked, but not mushy. Leave to cool, while you make up the shortcrust pastry, adding a little water if the egg is not sufficient to make it the correct wetness. Grease a pie dish and put in the *cool* filling, and put a pie-funnel in the centre. Roll out the pastry and cover the top of the pie dish with it. Make two sharp cuts in the centre of the pie to form a cross. Brush the pastry top with a little milk or beaten egg. Cook in a hot oven (Gas 7, 425°F) for about 20 minutes. Serve with custard.

Mrs Doris Archer's almond biscuits

Mrs Doris Archer is a great one for making biscuits and shortbread and her granddaughter Shula will make any excuse to call in at Glebe Cottage to try some of her Gran's home baking. The other day Mrs Doris called in the shop and the first thing she asked for was ground almonds. Well, I don't carry a big stock of them, because most of the villagers only buy almonds, ground or otherwise, at Christmas time, and just a few ask for them around Mothering Sunday, to make a simnell cake. But as this was the middle of summer, for once I couldn't oblige. But if she wasn't in a hurry, I told her, I could easily get some for the next week. You see she wanted to make a batch of almond biscuits. It's ever such an easy recipe to remember because it's just 4 oz of each ingredient.

4 oz caster sugar
4 oz margarine
4 oz plain flour

4 oz ground almonds
A few split almonds for decoration

Cream the sugar and the margarine together than add the flour and the almonds and mix to a make a good stiffish dough. Roll out thinly on a floured board, cut into rings and place a split almond on each biscuit. Place the biscuits on a greased baking sheet and cook near the top of the oven for about 20 minutes at Gas 4, 355°F. Remove from the baking sheet as soon as you fetch them out of the oven. Cool on a cake rack.

It's nice to have a few pots of strawberry jam in the larder, it comes in very handy to put on top of sweet scones, specially if you've got somebody coming to tea of a Sunday.

Strawberry jam

4 lb strawberries   4 lb sugar
2 lemons (3 if they are small and not very juicy)

Pick over the fruit, taking off any hulls or stalks, and lay them on a large meat dish. Sprinkle the juice of the lemons over the strawberries and 2 lb of the sugar and let them stand overnight. Pour off the juice that has formed on the dish into a preserving pan, add the rest of the sugar and bring up to the boil and continue to boil for 10 minutes. Now add the strawberries and cook for a further 15 minutes. Test to see if the jam will set by putting a small amount on a saucer. Leave to cool before giving it the finger test. Do this by pushing your finger over the surface, if a skin has formed then the jam is ready to be put into clean, warm jam pots. Put the wax discs on while the jam is hot, but don't put on the final cellophane pot cover until the jam is cold.

Some modern cooks swear by a bottle of liquid you can buy from the chemist to set their jam, but I'm a bit old-fashioned and likes to set mine with lemon juice and a bit of patience.

Dandelion wine

Of course this is the month of the dandelions and I can't abide to see all those lovely golden blooms growing and not to do anything with them. So I make gallons of dandelion wine, not that we drink it all. I suppose I give half my home-made wine away, to one and another. Any fêtes or bottle stalls or raffles that take place around here you can bet your life that there's several bottles of Martha's wine about. Even Harry Booker begs some to take to organizers in the hamlets he calls on as postman. Well, here's how I make mine. Some folks pull off the petals, but I just use the whole flower, as long as there's no green bits left on.

3 quarts flower heads (measured in a jug)	2 lemons
	1 orange
1 gallon water	1 oz yeast
4 lb sugar	

The flowers must be freshly picked, and be sure that there are not bits of stalks left on. Put the flower heads into a large crock, a plastic bucket will do if you haven't a large crock (old red stone wine pan). Boil up the gallon of water and pour over the flower heads, cover the pan with a cloth and leave for 3 days, stirring each day. After the third day, strain through butter muslin (or nylon curtain). Now put the juice into a large saucepan, add the sugar and the rinds of the lemons and orange and bring up to the boil and simmer gently for about 20 minutes. Tip this back into your crock and add the juice of the lemons and orange and when the wine is cool, but not cold – sprinkle the yeast on the top of it. Cover with a thick cloth and leave for 3 days. Strain again, pour into a demijohn, fix the air lock and leave until the wine stops working, when the bubbles stop. Bottle off and cork well. Try and leave the wine for at least 6 months before drinking it.

Sometimes, on fine summer mornings, I walk to the shop. I don't mean that I leave my old bike at home, no, I push it to work, so that I can pop back quick on it at dinner time. But it's so beautiful in the mornings and I saunter along 'drinking it all in' as my Joby says. There's so much to see and enjoy. The wild flowers this month are a picture, and I'm so glad that they have stopped cutting the grass on the sides of the road for a little while. At one time the local council seemed to wait until the white campions and the blue cranesbill and all the tufted veches were all out and then they would send a man and one of those machine things to cut them all down in their prime. Now they seem to cut the verge sides once early in June and again in late August, and by that time quite a lot of the wild flowers are gone over. I noticed that the giant convolvulous flowers are out, climbing all over the hedgerows. When we were small we used to pick them, turn them upside down, push a twig up in the middle of the flower and call them fairy parasols, and we made lovely little dolls from red poppies. All you did was pick a poppy, leaving the stalk about two inches long. Then you turned back the petals and tied it around the middle of the petals with a piece of grass, leaving the ends for arms, but the poor doll only had one leg, that bit of stalk. One morning when I was walking to work, some of Mrs Cattermole's children were wandering down the lane so I stopped and showed them how to make 'fairy parasols and one-legged poppy dolls', bless their little hearts, you'd have thought I'd given them the biggest treat in the world, it brought a lump to my throat to see the joy and delight in their eyes as I was making them. Now whenever they see me they say, 'Mrs Martha, when are you going to show us some more magic things?' But their mother soon shuts them up and says, 'Don't you take no notice of them Mrs Woodford, they'll worry the life out of you if you let um.'

Well, we've started enjoying the first early vegetables of the season, we've had young potatoes, broad beans and peas already. And I don't throw my peapods on the compost heap neither. Sometimes I make home-made wine with them, but mostly I make a nice summer soup.

Clear pea-pod soup

4 or 5 lb pea-pod shells	3 pints water
1 large onion	A few sprigs of mint
1 oz butter	Salt and pepper
	A little green colouring

Wash the shells and peel and slice the onion. Put the butter into a large saucepan along with the sliced onion and the pea shells and cook for a few minutes, stirring all the while. Now pour on the water and add the mint sprigs and salt and pepper to taste. Simmer this gently, stirring often, until the pea pods are nice and tender. Now strain the soup and return it to the saucepan, add a little green colouring and the soup is ready to eat. But if you should prefer a cream soup then all you need to do is to fry a nut of butter or bacon fat along with 2 tablespoons of flour, stirring all the while so it does not let it brown, then when you have a nice, smooth paste-like mixture add about $\frac{1}{3}$ pint of milk and tip this into the soup, bring it up to the boil again and it will give it a nice velvety softness.

Young Pat Archer came tearing into the shop the other day (she helps her husband Tony quite a lot and she always seems to be in a hurry). 'Martha,' she said, 'please have you some odds and ends of fat bacon you could let me have? You see,' she went on, 'I've invited Jennifer and Brian round for a meal tomorrow night and I thought I'd make some liver pâté for starters – you know, you serve it rolled up in a lettuce leaf, and it's so much cheaper to make than buying it. I've got plenty of chicken livers because I save them when we have a chicken, I just bung them in the freezer and use them when I want them.'

'Well,' I said, 'there's always some fat bits left over. How much did you want?'

'Oh, I reckon half a pound will be enough,' she replied. So I just slipped some odd bits into a bag and said that she could have them anyhow. I know that she and Tony have a bit of a job to make ends meet, especially when they are waiting for the milk cheque to come.

'Bless your heart, Martha,' she cried, 'I can pay for them,

we're not completely broke you know – bent yes, but not broke.' But I insisted that if she didn't have them I should just pass them on to somebody else, for free. So she went off quite happy, but she did say that if there was any left she would bring me a taste in the day after Jennifer and Brian had been. True to her word, she came in with quite a nice wedge of it, and the flavour was super. Well, here's how she made it.

Pat Archer's liver pâté

8 oz chicken livers	2 eggs, well beaten
1 good sized onion, sliced	Pepper
3 oz fat bacon, chopped	1 teaspoon garlic salt
1 clove garlic	

Put the liver and the sliced onion in a saucepan, along with a half a cup of water. Add the chopped up fat bacon and simmer gently until nicely cooked. Put the mixture through a mincer, add the clove of garlic and the eggs, well beaten, and the pepper and garlic salt. Mix well. Grease a baking tin and tip the mixture in to it, smoothing the top with a knife. Cover over with foil and then stand the tin in a larger baking tin containing water. Put into a warm oven (Gas 3, 335°F) and cook for about an hour. Take out of the oven but leave the foil on until quite cold.

Liver in batter

If you've got a nice bit of pig's or sheep's liver, here's a quick way of cooking it. First make a batter with 2 tablespoons of self-raising flour and enough cold water to make a good, thickish mix, then add a little salt. Put some lard in your frying pan, let it get good and hot. Cut the liver into smallish pieces and dip each piece into the batter and then fry quickly in the boiling fat. Lovely with chips.

Mrs Perkins's lamb cutlets

This recipe was given to me by Mrs Perkins. Of course Mrs P. was brought up at a time of great hard-up-ness and was taught to make the most of cheap joints of meat. Some folk would never think of using best end of neck of lamb for frying, but it certainly can be done.

Best end of neck of mutton	Dripping for frying
	Breadcrumbs
1 egg	Salt and pepper

Get your butcher to cut up the neck into cutlets. Cut off any surplus fat. Beat up the egg and put it on a plate. Put your breadcrumbs on another. Melt the dripping up in the frying pan, sprinkle the cutlets with salt and pepper and dip each one first in the egg and then in the breadcrumbs, covering the cutlets all over. Fry them until they are nicely browned on both sides, then turn the heat down for a few minutes so that the chops are cooked through. Serve with fresh home-grown peas and young potatoes.

Betty Tucker's bacon and egg tart

Betty Tucker is another Ambridge housewife who has known thin times, and she comes out with some very good ideas for economical meals. She reckons that this particular recipe which she passed on to me does her and Mike for two meals! The first day they eat it hot with vegetables and the next day they have the remainder with salad. I often make one of these during the summertime and if there's any left over I pack it up for my Joby's lunch.

The pastry
8 oz self-raising flour
4 oz margarine
1 small egg

The filling
4 streaky rashers
4 eggs
Salt and pepper

Make up the shortcrust pastry in the usual way and line a sandwich tin with half of it. Now lay the streaky rashers on and crack the eggs, keeping them whole on the top of the bacon. Add the salt and pepper to taste and then put the remaining pastry on the top. Brush the pastry over with a little milk and bake the tart in a nice hot oven (Gas 6, 400°F) for about 20 minutes. Turn down the heat to Gas 3, 335°F and cook for a further 5 minutes to make sure that the bacon is cooked.

We are very fortunate really having such a big garden, because it means that we are able to keep a few hens up at the far end. They keep us going in eggs and then they make us tasty meals when they have finished laying. Here's quite a good way to cook a fairly old bird, and the slow cooking suits me because it means I can put this sort of meal in the oven when I leave for work in the morning and it's done to a turn by dinnertime.

Don't forget, when you have the oven on for a long time try and slip in a milk pudding or maybe your next day's meal.

Chicken casserole

1 jointed chicken or hen	A sprig each of thyme, parsley and marjoram
1 oz dripping	½ pint stock or water
2 good sized onions	1 cup home-made (or bought) red wine
A little flour	1 tablespoon plain cornflour
Salt and pepper	2 or 3 tomatoes
2 oz mushrooms	

Melt the dripping in a frying pan. Peel and slice the onions and then fry them gently in the dripping. Put a little flour on a plate along with the salt and pepper. Dip each chicken joint in and then fry them lightly in the butter fat. Tip onions and chicken joints into a casserole. Cut up the tomatoes and mushrooms, tie the herbs in a little bundle and add these to chicken. Now cover with the stock and wine. Put the lid on the casserole and cook in a slowish oven (Gas 3, 335°F) for 3–3½ hours. Before dishing up mix the cornflour with a little water, now pour off about a cup of the chicken liquid and mix it with the cornflour. Bring up to the boil in a frying pan and then add it to the casserole and cook for a further 10 minutes.

Fillets of sole with mushroom sauce

4 fillets of sole	Salt and pepper to taste
Lemon juice	1 tablespoon milk

First skin the fillets, sprinkle with lemon juice and a little salt and pepper and then roll them up, securing them with a wooden cocktail stick. Place the fillets on a fireproof plate, cover with the milk and then place another plate on the top and steam the fillets over a saucepan of boiling water for about 20 minutes. Put the fillets on a hot dish and keep them warm while you make the sauce from the cooking liquor and mushrooms.

Mushroom sauce

1 oz margarine or butter	1 oz chopped mushrooms
1 oz flour	(cooked in a little butter for
Liquor the fish was	about 4 minutes)
cooked in	Salt and pepper
	Chopped parsley

Melt the fat in a frying pan and add the flour and cook for about 2 minutes (don't let the flour brown) stirring all the while. Add the liquor gradually and keep stirring so that the sauce is nice and smooth. Now add the cooked chopped mushrooms and salt and pepper to taste. Pour the sauce over the fish and sprinkle with the chopped parsley. Try and eat the fish at once.

One of young Neil's favourite teas on a Saturday was cauliflower cheese. Do you know when he first came to live with us he didn't know there was such a dish? He'd never tasted it in his life before. Anyhow, it's a good nourishing meal for anybody, because there's the goodness in the cauliflower, the cheese, butter and milk in the sauce, and of course he always ate several slices of bread and butter with it. I don't know if my recipe is any different to anybody else's, but it's a nice easy snack all the same.

Cauliflower cheese

Wash and trim the cauliflower, discarding all the green leaves. Cook it whole in boiling water for about 10–12 minutes. Drain.

Cheese sauce

1 oz butter	Pepper and salt
1 oz plain flour	A little made mustard
(or cornflour)	½ pint milk
4 tablespoons grated cheese (strong)	

Melt the butter in a saucepan. Take off the heat. Stir in the flour and cook very gently for a minute. Now add the grated cheese, salt and pepper, mustard and milk. Bring up to the boil, stirring all the while, until the cheese has melted. Place the cooked cauliflower in a pie dish or shallow baking tin and pour the sauce over. Sprinkle a little more grated cheese on the top and brown, either under the grill for a few moments or in a hot oven (Gas 7, 425°F) top shelf, for 2–3 minutes.

Sometimes the most simple recipes turn out to be the nicest. This unusual one was given to me by Peggy Archer and it's a good way of using up cream that might have passed its best, I don't mean gone right off but perhaps not nice enough to eat with fruit.

Raspberry robber

1 lb raspberries	1 tablespoon flour
1 cup cream	1 tablespoon caster sugar
2 eggs	

Place the raspberries in a fireproof dish and put them into a warm oven for about 10 minutes when the juice will begin to run. Take the dish from the oven. In a separate bowl put the cream, eggs, flour and sugar and whip them up together. Pour this over the raspberries and bake for about 20 minutes at Gas 4, 355°F until the top is tawny brown.

Ripe raspberry special

Here's another pudding made with raspberries, only this one doesn't require any cooking. Well, you can't call warming a drop of fruit juice cooking, can you? This is what you need to make a lovely light pudding:

¼ pint raspberry purée	¼ pint cream
½ oz gelatine	¼ lb caster sugar
2 egg whites	

Put ¼ lb ripe raspberries into a blender and blend for 2 minutes. Warm a small quantity of this and sprinkle the gelatine on the top and put aside for a few minutes. Beat the egg whites and the cream together. Now mix together the raspberry purée, the now softened gelatine, the sugar and the egg whites and cream and whip all up till fairly stiff. Put into sundae type glasses and put into the fridge for a little while. Before serving decorate the top of each glass with about 3 raspberries.

Gooseberry joy

This is another very tasty pudding to make while the gooseberries are at their best. If you have a sweet tooth you may need more sugar than stated.

1½ lb gooseberries, topped and tailed
3-4 oz sugar
A little water
2 oz butter or margarine
3 oz breadcrumbs
2 eggs

First put the gooseberries into a saucepan with the sugar and water and cook them gently for about 10 minutes, stirring all the while, until the fruit is nice and soft. Stir in the butter or margarine and put aside to cool. Then add the breadcrumbs and beat up the eggs and add them also. Put this mixture into a well greased pie dish and bake in a moderate oven (Gas 4, 355°F) for about 35-40 minutes. This is lovely eaten hot or cold.

Jill's special cake made for Doris Archer's birthday

It's Mrs Doris Archer's birthday this month and all the family usually meet at Glebe Cottage to drink her health – not for a party, but just to have a drink and some refreshments. This year Jill made a special cake for Mrs Doris; for a change it wasn't a rich fruit one and everyone said it was beautiful.

½ lb butter
½ lb caster sugar
6 eggs, beaten
¾ lb self-raising flour
1 teaspoon baking powder
2 pinches salt
½ lb walnuts, chopped
¼ lb crystallized pineapple, chopped
¼ lb flaked almonds
2 lemons
1 orange

Cream the fat and sugar together then add the beaten eggs. In a separate bowl put the flour, baking powder and salt.

Chop the walnuts and pineapple and almonds. Now fold the flour into the creamed butter etc., and then add the nuts and pineapple. Now grate in the lemon and orange rind and add the juice from these.

Line an 8" cake tin with greaseproof paper and put the cake mixture in. Place in a pre-heated oven (Gas 3, 335°F) for 2½ hours. When cooked take the cake from the oven, remove the greaseproof paper and cool on a cake rack.

For the butter icing

4 oz butter	4 tablespoons brandy
12 oz icing sugar	A few walnuts for decoration

Place the butter in a mixing bowl and stand the bowl over a saucepan of very hot water and beat in the icing sugar, then add the brandy. Continue beating until a nice thick consistency is reached. Take the mixing bowl off the hot water and spread the icing quickly on to the cold cake. Decorate with halved walnuts.

Drop or girdle scones

Drop scones or girdle scones are very easy to make and they cook in about 4 minutes. Sometimes when folk pay us a surprise visit on a Sunday, I whip up some batter quickly while the kettle's aboiling for a cuppa, then while the visitors are supping the tea I get out my girdle, or griddle, pan as some people call them, and cook some. Oh they go down lovely spread with butter, home-made jam, honey or syrup. You can eat them hot or cold, but we like them best piping hot.

4 oz plain flour	A pinch of salt
½ teaspoons baking powder	½ beaten egg
½ oz caster sugar	¼ pint milk

Put the flour into a bowl along with the baking powder, sugar and salt. Beat up the half egg along with the milk and add this to the flour, etc., and mix together to make a thinish batter. Now get your girdle pan (you can also cook these on a hot plate of an electric stove) good and hot, wipe over with a little butter paper and then drop a good dessertspoonful of the mixture on to the hot gridle. Cook for about 2 minutes, until the top is covered with tiny bubbles, turn over and brown the other side. Line a dish with a clean tea towel and as each batch is cooked transfer them to this, and the scones will keep hot and moist until you are ready to eat them.

Mrs Doris Archer's shortbread
(Shula's favourite)

8 oz butter	12 oz plain flour
4 oz caster sugar	Pinch of salt

Put the butter and the sugar into a bowl and knead together until quite soft. Then gradually add the flour, sifted with the pinch of salt, still kneading with the hands until all is completely mixed. Grease a tin, lightly dusting it over with flour and place the mixture in it, pressing it down with the palm of the hand or rolling it very lightly with a milk bottle or rolling pin. Mark the edges with a fork and prick the surface all over too. Now place in a slowish oven (Gas 3, 335°F) on the middle shelf and bake for about an hour until the shortbread is a pale golden colour. Take from the oven and sprinkle with a little caster sugar. Mark out into squares or oblongs, whichever you wish, but don't remove from the tin until cold.

I often think of dear Mrs Turvey who used to live in Ambridge, what a splendid old lady she was too. Emily Tarbutt was her companion, she used to do most of the gardening and Mrs Turvey the cooking. But it's at this time of year that I am reminded of her most because it was she who first told me, 'Never ever boil your raspberries for jam making, Mrs Woodford. I never do, my dear mother always impressed on me to make my raspberry preserve – she never called it jam you know – by simply warming the sugar and fruit.'

Well I'd never heard of making it like that, I've always made mine like I make any other sort of jam; mind you my Joby never did like pippy jam, because the pips gets under his plate. But made the way that Mrs Turvey told me, well you don't seem to get the pips hard at all, and the flavour is just like eating fresh picked raspberries. You don't lose the lovely red colour either, like you do in ordinary jam making. And it's so simple it's hardly believable.

Mrs Turvey's raspberry preserve

4 lb raspberries
4 lb sugar

Put the fruit on to a large flat meat dish and put the sugar on to another one. Set your oven temperature at Gas 3, 335°F and place the dishes near the top of the oven. When the fruit juice begins to run, which will be after about ¼ hour, take out the fruit and tip it into a large saucepan, followed by the sugar. Put over a very low flame for about 5 minutes and beat the fruit and sugar together with a wooden spoon until the sugar has dissolved. Pot at once in hot jam jars and seal in the usual way and it will keep as well and as long as any other jam.

Mary Pound's blackcurrant jam

Mary Pound is not very fond of cooking, but she does like to make jam from the fruit which grows in their garden.

She came into the shop the other day, mid morning it was. 'Whatever are you doing in here at this time of the morning Mary?' I said. 'I'd have thought you'd have wanted to get on with cutting that second crop of grass of yours that you were on about yesterday.'

'Well, you knows me,' she said, 'I'd rather be doing that but me damn blackcurrants be ripe and I must make some jam, good for colds in the wintertime it is. Put a good spoonful in a cup of boiling water, stir it well and drink it down, that'll cure any cold, my Ken and me swears by it. So I wants about nine pounds of sugar,' she went on, 'that took me all last evening to pick the blessed things. 'Course if our Marlene was anything like she'd have come over and made it for me.' Off she went with the sugar, still grumbling because she had to stay in and make the jam.

3 lb sugar
1 pint water to every 1½ lb blackcurrants

Take off any stalks and the brown ends of the fruit before putting them into a large saucepan, add the water and bring up to the boil and cook for 20 minutes. Take off the heat, add the sugar and boil up again for about 7 minutes. Test in the usual way, but blackcurrant jam sets well anyway. Pour into warm jam pots and cover when cold. Made like this the jam should keep for at least 2 years.

Mixed fruit wine

When the soft fruit have passed their best, and when I think I've made enough jam and jelly, then I use what I call 'the tail end fruit' to make a lovely mixed fruit wine. What I do is pick the last of the raspberries, gooseberries, black and redcurrants and even manage to find a few strawberries to go in. I make the fruit up to about 4 lb, which I pick over, throwing away any rotten fruit. Then I put them in a large crock. To this I add a gallon of boiling water, and leave it for 3 days, stirring each day. Then I strain it off, pour back the juice into the crock, stir in 4 lbs or sugar and the juice and rind of 2 lemons, and sprinkle on $\frac{1}{2}$ oz yeast. Cover well with a thick cloth and leave for a week. Then I strain again, pour the wine into a demijohn, fix the airlock and leave until all fermentation has stopped. Then I bottle it off in the usual way. This makes a very nice red-coloured sweet wine, and is a great favourite of ours.

AUGUST

There's such a lot of activity in the village during this month. All day long tractors with trailers piled high with grain go puffing from the harvest fields to the corn driers. Jethro calls by quite often to swap empty lemonade bottles for full ones. I said to Jethro that I'd have thought he'd have preferred cold tea, it's a much better thirst quencher than any bottled stuff, and I'll bet his old dad drank nothing else during harvest time. He agreed with me, but said his Lizzie always drained the pot dry anyway and there was never any left for him to pour into a bottle if he wanted to. But it's the speed of the harvest work that I can't get over: in the morning you might see a field of corn, ripe and golden in the hot sunshine, and by evening time all that's left is the shaven stubble, even the straw bales have been cleared away.

Christine Johnson came into the shop the other morning asking for some good thick slices of gammon bacon. 'Ah,' I said, 'what tasty dish are you concocting tonight?'

'Well,' she replied, 'Paul and I thought we'd spoil ourselves by having one of our favourite meals, baked ham and pineapple, that's if you have some gammon bacon and of course a tin of pineapple, and Queen of puddings* for afters.' Well, thankfully I was able to supply her with both the gammon and the pineapple.

'But,' I said, handing her the groceries, 'I'd certainly like to know how you cook this special dish.'

'Bless your heart, Martha, it's that easy, here give me a scrap of paper and I'll jot it down for you.' Well, here it is, and it certainly sounds lovely though I've not cooked it myself yet. But I must ask her what else she ate with it.

Christine Johnson's gammon and pineapple special

3 gammon rashers cut thick	6 cloves
	A little made mustard
2 tablespoons demerara sugar	1 small tin pineapple rings
	1 dessertspoon cornflour

Have the gammon cut about ¼″ thick. Cut off the rind and snip the fat edge in a few places. Rub the surface of the meat with half the sugar and the made mustard. Stick the cloves, two in each gammon. Place them in a meat dish and cover with the juice from the tin of pineapple. Cover and cook for about ½ hour at (Gas 4, 355°F) Cut the pineapple rings in half, spread them with the remaining brown sugar and brown for a few minutes under a hot grill. Now strain off the juice from the cooked gammon and thicken it with cornflour. To serve place the gammon on to a hot dish, pour over the sauce and decorate with the pineapple.

*See page 147 for the recipe.

Jill Archer's 'ketchops'

It was Mrs Jill Archer who told me of this very different way to cook pork chops. She had made it up herself. You see she is what she calls 'quite inventive' with her cooking, and is always trying out different ways of cooking things and adding the most unusual ingredients to the dishes. I cooked us a couple of pork chops the way she had told me, serving them up with slices of lemon, to which my Joby remarked, 'Whatever is this slice of lemon doing on me chop, I thought lemons were for squeezing on pancakes'. So I had to whip the lemon off his chop pretty quick, but I kept mine on and the flavour was smashing. Mind you we did eat ours with mashed potatoes and spring cabbage, whereas Mrs Phil serves hers garnished with cress or parsley and served with croutons.

4 pork chops, about ¾″ thick	2 tablespoons brown sugar
A little dripping for frying	6 tablespoons tomato ketchup or sauce
8 thin slices lemon	Water

First of all put the dripping in a frying pan, and brown the chops on both sides. Pour off any excess fat. Place a piece of lemon on top of each chop. Now mix together the brown sugar, ketchup and water and pour this mixture over the chops. Put lid on pan and simmer slowly for about 30 minutes, basting chops occasionally. Now skim off any excess fat and simmer for 10 minutes more. Serve the chops on a hot dish with a fresh slice of lemon on top of each and ketchup mixture round the chops. Garnish with cress or parsley.

Shepherd's pie

I suppose that shepherd's pie is the most popular way of using up bits of cold meat, whether it's beef or lamb or cold chicken. Mary Pound puts all sorts of vegetables in hers –

mashed carrots, peas or parsnips as well as potatoes. But then I expect she does that for convenience, cooking it all together I mean. But we like it best made with meat, potatoes and onion, and a slice of stale bread.

$\frac{1}{2}$–$\frac{3}{4}$ lb any odd meat	Pepper
A good sized onion	1 lb boiled mashed potatoes
1 slice stale bread	Dripping
Cup of gravy	

First mince up your meat, along with a good sized onion. Lastly put a slice of stale bread through the mincer and mix this up well with the meat; this makes it go much further and also cleans out any meat left in the mincer. Mix the mince up well with the gravy, add a good sprinkling of pepper and put it in the bottom of a pie dish or meat tin. Cover the meat with the mashed potatoes and mark the top of the potatoes by drawing a fork across the top of them. Dot with dripping and cook for about 20 minutes in a hot oven (Gas 7, 425°F) until nicely browned on the top. Serve with Brussels sprouts.

Tom Forrest came into the shop today, grinning all over his face. 'Now what's pleasing you?' I asked him. 'I've brought you something special, Martha,' he said, and from a small hessian bag he fetched a young leveret. And although he's no longer head gamekeeper, he still gets hold of some game now and then. He went on to say that Gordon Armstrong had given him a couple of leverets the day before, one he and Prue were having for dinner that day and the other one he brought along for Joby and me, knowing how fond we are of them. And although of course they are young and tender, I like to cook mine in a casserole, and I know this is how Prue cooks hers.

Leveret casserole

1 leveret	½ lb mushrooms
1 tablespoon flour	½ lb onions
Salt and pepper	⅛ teaspoon each chopped
2 oz margarine or dripping	parsley, thyme and marjoram
	½ milk or milk and water

The hare will most likely be paunched when you buy it, if not, it's a simple, but bloody job. Here's how you do it:

Lay the hare on its back. Using a sharp knife or razor blade, make a long slit down its stomach (from ribs downwards). Place the hand inside and draw out the intestines. At this point catch some of the blood from the animal as some folks like to use it in the cooking of jugged hare, but I never do. Now wipe the inside with a damp cloth. The animal is now ready for skinning.

Lay the hare on its back and cut off the four skuts (feet). Pull the skin away from the left leg, then with the right hand pull the leg out of the skin (as you would take a small child's arm from a coat). You will find that the skin will come away quite easily. Now treat the right leg the same. Turn the animal over on to its stomach, just nick the fleshy part of the tail with a knife. Pull the skin with the left hand and the hare with the right till you reach the jumpers* and push these

*When talking about a hare back legs are always called so, but front ones are known as jumpers.

through just as you did the back legs. At this point I cut the head off (leaving it in the skin) but some folks cook it along with the rest. It you are going to cook the hare whole just put it to soak in cold salt water for about an hour. But if you are cooking it in joints then this is the time to cut it up, making three joints from the back. Keep the liver and heart and cook it along with the rest of the meat.

(Skin a rabbit in just the same way.)

Cut the leveret up into joints and soak for a few minutes in cold salt water. Then dry them well and dip each piece in seasoned flour. Melt the margarine (or dripping) in a frying pan and fry each joint for a few minutes on both sides. Place the joints in a casserole and then fry the mushrooms and onions and tip them into the casserole; also tip in the remaining seasoned flour and finely chopped herbs, then add the milk and water. Place a lid on the casserole and put into a warm oven (Gas 4, 355°F) for about 1 hour. Turn down heat to (Gas 2, 310°F) and cook for a further 20 minutes, when the meat should be nice and tender. Serve with young potatoes and runner beans or summer cabbage.

Of course young rabbit can be cooked just the same. But it will be a very different flavour from the leveret.

Fish pie

This is one of Mrs Perkins's specials. We do get a van come round the village once a week bringing fresh fish and it's surprising the people who buy from it. 'Course the villagers can always get frozen fish from me, but I do think you need a bit of fresh to make a pie with.

½ lb white fish, cooked and flaked
½ lb mashed potatoes
1 oz butter

A little milk
Pepper and salt
A cup of breadcrumbs

Parsley sauce
1 oz butter
1 oz plain flour
½ pint milk

Salt and pepper
A little chopped parsley

Make up the sauce by melting the butter in a saucepan, then stir in the flour, add the milk and season with salt and pepper, stirring all the while. Cook for about 3 minutes until nice and thick. Add the chopped parsley.

First remove any skin and bone from the cooked fish and then flake up with a fork and mix in the parsley sauce. Place this mixture in a greased pie dish. Mash the potatoes with the butter and a drop of milk until they are nice and fluffy, then spread them on top of the fish. Sprinkle the top of the pie with the breadcrumbs and dot a little more butter on the top. Bake in a hot oven (Gas 7, 425°F) for about 20 minutes.

This is a nice time of the year with the runner beans coming in and plenty of tomatoes and young tender marrows. Here's a nice tasty supper dish using marrow, tomatoes and cheese and it's so simple to do.

Marrow, tomato and cheese bake

1 young marrow	1 lb tomatoes
Salt and pepper	4–6 oz cheese, grated
1 oz butter	

Choose a marrow about 12–15" long. Peel it, cut it in half lengthwise and scrape out the pips. Lay the two halves side by side in a meat tin, sprinkle with salt and pepper and dot with the butter and cover with lid. Put into a warm oven (Gas 3, 335°F) for about ½ hour. While the marrow is cooking take the tomatoes and pour boiling water over them; leave for about 2 minutes. Take out of the water and remove the skins, slice the tomatoes quite thickly and sprinkle with salt and pepper. Also grate the cheese. Take the marrow from the oven, but keep it in the meat tin, lay the sliced tomatoes on the top of the marrow and then sprinkle the cheese on the top. Put the oven temperature up to (Gas 5, 380°F), slip the dish back in and cook for about 10 minutes, when the cheese will have melted and began to turn a lightish brown. Eat at once with bread and butter. Lovely.

Mrs Perkins's tasty snack

I was telling Mrs P. how to make this last dish and then she turned round and told me of another tasty snack using tomatoes.

½ lb ripe tomatoes	1 egg
2 oz butter	Hot buttered toast
Salt and pepper	

First plunge the tomatoes in boiling water for a few moments. Then take them out, peel them and slice them quite thinly.

Melt the butter in a saucepan and cook the tomatoes in this until they are soft and mushy. Sprinkle with salt and pepper. Beat up the egg and then add it to the saucepan and stir until the mixture thickens. Pile on to the hot buttered toast.

Mushrooms the country way

We had our first mushrooms of the season today. Joby was walking across a field where the corn had been cut a few days before, and blow me if he didn't pick about a pound of lovely young mushrooms. I soon had them peeled and in the frying pan I can tell you. We like them fried first in a little butter, adding plenty of pepper and salt, then I sprinkle about a tablespoon of flour on them and cook for a further 5 minutes stirring all the while, then I add about a cup and a half of milk and bring up to the boil again until the mushrooms are done and the pan is filled with a lovely thick grey sauce. I'll bet you'll never just fry them in bacon fat once you've tried my method.

We don't see a lot of Lilian and Ralph Bellamy these days, but when they do pay a visit to Ambridge, Lilian usually comes into the shop to see me, just to say hello. Sometimes she'll buy a few sweets – especially if young James is with her – although she doesn't think that children should really eat sweets and rations young James out with things like barley sugar or liquorice. The last time she came in she said, 'Martha, I know you like to try out new recipes. I wonder if you'd like to know how to make a simple little sweet, one that we often have back home in Guernsey. The joy of it is that it doesn't need cooking, Ralph calls it Guernsey Goo,' she went on, 'but the proper name is "Maria's roll", and you can use it as a pudding or as a cake, whichever you like.'

Maria's roll

18 or 20 ginger biscuits
4 tablespoons sherry or
    cointreau
½ pint double cream
Some split roasted
    almonds
An oval dish

First dampen each biscuit with the sherry or cointreau, but don't make them too soggy. Whip the cream until it's nice and thick and use about half of it to sandwich the biscuits together, placing them on the oval serving dish so that they look like a swiss roll. Pour any remaining sherry over the roll and then completely cover it with the rest of the cream. Put the roll in the fridge for 3–4 hours. Blanch and skin the almonds and split in half. Place them on a baking sheet and put them in a warm oven (Gas 4, 355°F) until they are nicely browned. When you are ready to serve the pudding decorate with the almonds, so that it looks like a hedgehog.

Ambridge fruit loaf

Quite a lot of the Ambridge wives make their own bread, and this is a great favourite. I usually make a couple of loaves while I'm about it, because they keep well if you wrap them in foil and store them in an airtight tin. I think it was Mrs Dan Archer who gave me the recipe.

6 oz self-raising flour	4 oz mixed dried fruit
3 oz soft brown sugar	½ teaspoon mixed spice
¼ teaspoon salt	1 cup water

Simply mix all the dry ingredients together well, and then add nearly a cup of cold water. Mix and pour this mixture into a greased loaf tin. Bake in a moderate oven (Gas 5, 380°F) for ¾ hour. Take out of the oven and wrap the loaf in a clean cloth and leave until it's quite cold. Wrap the bread in foil and leave for at least 3 days before cutting. Then spread very generously with butter. Lovely for Sunday tea.

Christine's Queen of puddings

Well, this is how Christine Johnson makes her Queen of puddings, and I certainly think it's the best recipe I've tried.

½ pint milk	3 oz breadcrumbs
1 oz butter	2 eggs
Grated rind of 1 lemon	2 tablespoons jam
½ teaspoon vanilla essence	(strawberry if possible)
2½ oz caster sugar	

Put the milk in a saucepan along with the butter, lemon rind, essence and 1 oz of sugar. Bring up to the boil, pour over the breadcrumbs, and mix well. Separate the eggs and stir the yolks into this mixture. Put into a pie dish, and bake for about 25 minutes in a moderate oven (Gas 4, 355°F). Take from the oven and spread the top of the pudding with the jam which has been gently warmed. Beat up the egg whites along with the rest of the caster sugar till nice and stiff, pile this on the top of the pudding and return to the oven, this time have the setting much lower (Gas 1, 290°F) and cook until the meringue topping is light brown and quite firm to touch. Eat the pudding hot.

Banbury cakes

If you ever get any stale fruit cake left in the tin here's a good way to use it up. Banbury cakes aren't half as difficult to make as some people think and they keep very well in a close fitting tin.

Rough puff pastry	*Filling*
8 oz plain flour	3 oz stale cake crumbs
1 teaspoon salt	2 oz soft brown or demerara
A squeeze of lemon juice	sugar
8 oz lard	3 oz soft margarine
Water to mix (about	2 oz currants
¼ pint)	1 level tablespoon mixed spice

Make pastry by sifting flour into basin; add salt, lemon juice and lard cut up into smallish cubes. Add water gradually, mixing with a knife. Roll out into a floured board, fold and roll again. Put pastry into the fridge for about 1 hour. Then take out and repeat the rolling and folding before returning it to the fridge for another ½ hour.

To make the filling, mix all ingredients together. Roll out pastry *very* lightly and cut (using a saucer) into rounds, then form into ovals with fingers. Pile the filling on, damp the edges, and pinch together. Now turn each Banbury cake over on to a floured board and flatten the cakes. Brush tops with the white of an egg and sprinkle with caster sugar. Lay the cakes on a greased baking sheet and bake them in hot oven (Gas 8, 450°F) for 25–30 minutes. Cool on a wire tray.

Gingerbread

It's old Walter's birthday this month and as usual Dan and Doris asked him round to Glebe Cottage for a bite to eat on the great day. Afterwards Walter headed for the Bull where Sid and Tom pulled his leg and pretended that they didn't know that it was the old fellow's birthday. Polly had made him a lovely cake, of course she had to watch what she put in it because Walter has to be a bit careful what he eats, because he's a diabetic. But she made him one almost like the one Jill made for Doris's birthday last month, only Polly left out the nuts because she thought that they mightn't be good for him. She put one candle in the centre and just as Walter was about to leave the Bull in disgust because nobody had bought him a drink, in comes Polly carrying the cake and everybody started to sing 'Happy Birthday'. Joby was there and he said that tears ran down the old fellow's cheeks, he was so overcome.

I usually make a slab of gingerbread as a standby, it's the sort that keeps for weeks as long as it's wrapped in foil, even then, if some of it gets a bit stale you can use it up for pudding by just covering it with thick hot custard. And here's how the gingerbread is made.

1 lb self-raising flour	½ lb margarine or butter
1 heaped tablespoon ground ginger	½ lb golden syrup
	½ lb black treacle
1 heaped teaspoon mixed spice	2 small eggs, well beaten
	¼ pint milk
½ lb soft brown sugar	

Sift the flour, ginger and mixed spice together in a bowl. Then put the sugar, margarine, syrup and treacle in a saucepan and gently warm through, but do not allow it to get too hot. Mix all the ingredients together, including the eggs and milk, and mix well. At this point it will be very runny but don't worry, that's how it should be. Pour into a greased and lined meat tin and bake in a slow oven (Gas 3, 350°F) for 1¼–1½ hours. Allow the gingerbread to cool in the tin for 5 minutes, remove paper and then cool on a cake rack. When quite cold, wrap in aluminium foil and leave at least 3 days before eating.

Sometimes I make a slab of this type gingerbread and give it to Walter. I put a bit less ground ginger and mixed pudding spice in the one I make for him. But we like ours quite 'gingery' so I put a heaped tablespoon in. Of course this could be varied according to people's individual taste.

This month the beetroot are at their best, nice and small and young. I usually make some beet chutney in August. It's such a beautiful flavour and comes out a nice rich ruby colour. And this is what you need to fill between four and five pound-pots. If you are lucky enough to grow your own beet, onions and apples it turns out very cheap to make.

Beetroot chutney

3 lb beetroot	½ teaspoon ground ginger
1½ lb apples	½ lb sugar
2 large onions	Juice of 1 lemon
1 pint vinegar	½ teaspoon salt

Boil the beetroot in salted water for 1½ hours; when cool skin them and cut into small cubes. Then peel and chop the apples and onions and boil in the vinegar for 20 minutes, adding the salt, ground ginger, sugar and lemon juice. Add the beetroot cubes and boil up again for 15 minutes; when cool put into jars and tie down. This can be eaten within a couple of weeks, but will keep all winter long.

Plum chutney

This month and next is specially busy for the housewife, with all the pickling and chutney to be done, but it's worth all the hard work because its so much cheaper to make your own. If there's a good crop of plums I make both plum wine, which is like port, and plum chutney as well as the usual plum jam, which is my Joby's favourite; he loves it on a bit of plain suet pudding or on a steamed pudding. Anyhow, here's the way that Joby's mother made her plum chutney, because that's where I found the recipe, in *her* little book.

4 lb ripe plums (red if possible)	1 lb sugar
1 lb sharp cooking apples	1 oz pickling spice (tied in a piece of muslin)
2 lb onions	½ lb sultanas
1 lb tomatoes	½ teaspoon each ground
1 pint vinegar	ginger and cinnamon

Cut the plums in half and take out the stones. Peel apples, onions and tomatoes and chop them all into cubes. Put the vinegar, sugar, ginger and cinnamon into a large saucepan along with the bag of pickling spice and bring almost up to the boil. Take off the heat and add the plums, apples, onions, tomatoes and sultanas and cook very gently for one and a half hours, stirring often. Bottle and tie down in the usual way.

Walter Gabriel's plum wine

This recipe for plum wine came from Walter Gabriel, one of his old granny's concoctions I shouldn't wonder.

4 lb ripe plums	4 lb sugar
1 gallon water	½ oz yeast

First cut up the fruit quite roughly, place it in a large crock or plastic bucket and pour over the gallon of boiling water. Cover and leave for 5 days, but remember to stir it at least once a day. Strain through muslin or nylon curtaining. Now pour the liquid back into the crock and stir in the 4 lbs sugar and keep stirring until you can feel that all the sugar has dissolved. Sprinkle the yeast on the top (mind you Walter still puts his on a piece of toast and then floats it on the top of the wine, but it really isn't necessary). Cover again and leave for a week. Then strain the wine again, pour into a demijohn, fix the airlock and leave until all the working has stopped. Then bottle off into bottles. Best kept for a year when the wine will look and taste almost like port.

I know that September is really here when I see the swallows and martins crowding on the telegraph wires, chirping and chattering away, no doubt planning the exact day of their journey to a warmer country.

The village street seems very quiet now that all the corn harvest has been gathered in. Young Neil called in to see us the other night and he said that all Mr Phil had to get in was the potatoes and sugar beet.

The hedgerow up from our cottage is smothered with blackberries. Come Sunday I shall take off with my basket and walking stick and gather some. I like to make the most of any 'free' harvest that's going. We've had our fair share of mushrooms this month, and some mornings my Joby's been up at five o'clock picking them. I don't think there's anything nicer than finding fresh dewy wet mushrooms – unless its eating 'um.

Of course the big event in Ambridge this months is the produce show, and all the chat in the shop is about 'who's going to put this and that in', and always somebody thinks their potatoes are bigger and their beans longer than anybody else's. Still, we shall see on the great day. I know I've got some very nice bottled fruit that I'm showing and my raspberry preserve looks and tastes lovely, so I shall put a pot of that in too.

The home-made wine section is always very well supported and there's a bit of friendly rivalry between Walter and myself as to whose wine is the clearest and the best tasting. But last year we were both surprised when Christine Johnson beat us all with her rose petal wine. She was so glad when she heard that she got top points for it that she opened it there and then and we all had a drop. It had a very very nice flavour (if that's the right word for good tasting wine) and was a nice delicate shade of pink.

It's surprising what a lot of flavour can be got from a few bacon bones. These, along with some lentils and a few sticks of celery, make a lovely tasty soup.

Lentil soup

½ lb lentils
2 sticks celery
1 good sized onion
A few bacon bones

Salt and pepper (you may not need much salt as the bacon is often a bit salty)
1 tablespoon white wine vinegar

First soak the lentils in cold water for 12 hours, then strain. Now chop up the celery and onion and put them in a saucepan along with the bacon bones, 2 pints cold water and the lentils. Add salt and pepper to taste and simmer gently until the lentils are cooked. Stir in the vinegar and serve. You can remove the bones before dishing up if you wish.

Turnip soup

Turnip soup makes quite a nice change, because the flavour is very different to any other country soup.

About 6 medium sized turnips (1 to 1½ lb)	½ teaspoon sugar
1 oz butter	2 pints boiling water
Salt and pepper to taste	1 egg yolk
	1 tablespoon 'top of the milk'

Peel and slice the turnips, put the butter in the saucepan, toss in the turnips and fry them for about 5 minutes, stirring them all the while. Now add the salt, pepper and sugar and pour on the boiling water and simmer until the turnips are really soft. Mash them well against the side of the saucepan (or put through a blender if you have one). Beat the egg yolk and the top of the milk together and gently stir into the soup, just before serving.

Sometimes the cheaper joints of meat need a bit different cooking than just plain roasting. One way of doing this is to pot roast it, because this way you get all the goodness and flavour of the meat and vegetables blended together. Mary Pound is a great one for pot roasting. She always says that she's got no time for fancy cooking and once a pot roast is prepared and in the oven (or saucepan) whichever you cook it, it needs no other attention till you dish it up.

Mary Pound's pot roast

1 to 1½ lb top or silver side (beef)
1 oz butter
3 carrots

3 good sized onions
1 turnip
A few stalks of celery
Salt and pepper

Melt the butter in a pan and fry the meat quickly, browning it on both sides. Take from the pan and put on one side. Peel all the vegetables, cut them up into cubes, toss them into the frying pan and cook for a few minutes. Add pepper and salt. Place the vegetables in a heavy saucepan and lay the meat on the bed of vegetables and cover all with about a gill of water. Put on a tight-fitting lid and place over a very low heat on the top of the cooker, and cook very gently for about 2 hours. This can also be cooked in the oven, in a casserole for about 2 hours at Gas 3, 335°F. But when I get a joint that looks as if it might be tough, I don't risk baking it, so I slice it up into thick slices and fry them quickly on both sides to seal in the goodness, lay them in a meat tin, add salt and pepper, cover completely with plenty of sliced onion and a knob or two of dripping and about a cup of brown gravy. I then cover with a lid and put into a warm oven (Gas 4, 355°F) and cook for about 2 hours. Cooked in this way the meat will be beautifully tender and the onions soft and juicy.

George Barford came sailing into the shop this morning with a couple of lovely young rabbits for me. He said that Tom Forrest had told him that whenever he's anything like this to spare he was to bring it in to me. Of course Tom is now well settled in at the garden centre, and very happy too by all accounts, but he still keeps in touch with George and Gordon.

On Sunday I shall make a nice rabbit pie with bacon and mushrooms in and then later on in the week I'll no doubt make a stew with the other one. If I put it in the solid fuel stove oven before I go to work one morning that'll be done to a turn by the time Joby and I get home at half-past twelve.

Rabbit stew

1 rabbit	1 oz dripping
1 tablespoon flour	1 or 2 onions
Salt and pepper	A sprig each of parsley,
3 oz fat bacon	thyme and majoram
	A couple of cloves

After skinning the rabbit cut it up into joints. Put the flour on a plate, season well with salt and pepper and dip each joint into it. Cut the bacon up small and lightly fry it in the dripping. Then take out and put in a casserole. Now fry the rabbit joints, browning them on both sides. Add the peeled sliced onion to this and tip it all into the casserole. Tie the herbs and cloves up in a bit of muslin, pop this and the flour that's left on the plate into the casserole and fill up with water just to cover all the contents. Put on a lid and cook in a slow oven (Gas 3, 335°F) for 3–4 hours. If you like a brown gravy, then add some gravy browning or a couple of meat cubes towards the end of the cooking. The little bag of herbs can be easily taken out before serving.

Fish cakes

By making fish cakes you can make a small amount of fish go a long way.

½ lb cooked fish (cod or fresh haddock)
A little butter
Salt and pepper
1 tablespoon chopped parsley

1 lb mashed potato
1 tablespoon flour
1 egg, beaten
2 oz breadcrumbs
A little fat for frying

White sauce
¼ oz butter
¼ oz flour

¼ pint milk
Salt and pepper

Dot the fish with a little butter and season with salt and pepper. Cover and cook for about 20 minutes at Gas 4, 355°F. Then take the fish from the oven, remove any skin and bone and flake it with a fork. Make the sauce by melting the butter in a pan, add the flour and stir for a couple of minutes, then add the milk gradually, stirring all the time until it thickens. Season to taste.

Beat the sauce into the fish, add the parsley, mashed potato, and salt and pepper to taste. Then leave this mixture to get cool. Now flour the hands well and divide the mixture into little cakes. Then dip them first into beaten egg and then into breadcrumbs and fry in hot fat until golden brown.

Nora was telling me the other day that there's one vegetable that George would eat every day, if he had the chance, and that's onions. But best of all he likes them stuffed, with sage and onion too! I usually make a stuffing with parsley and thyme when we have them. Well, there's no accounting for taste is there, so here's how Nora cooks hers.

Stuffed baked onions

4 good sized onions   Fat for baking

Stuffing

½ lb grated onion (and what   1 teaspoon sage
you take out of the centre   Salt and pepper
of the larger onions)   Dripping to bind
½ lb breadcrumbs

First skin the onions and place in a saucepan, cover with cold water, add a pinch of salt and cook for about 20 minutes. Drain off the water. Put the onions upright in a meat tin. Carefully take out the centre of them and add this to the stuffing, which should be all mixed up together. Stuff as much as you possibly can into the centre of the onions. If there's any left over make it into balls and cook along with the onions which should be dotted with the dripping before putting them into a warm oven (Gas 4, 355°F) for about ½–¾ hour. Be sure and baste the onions a couple of times during cooking.

Potato pancakes

This recipe makes a nice change for Saturday tea. Eaten with a couple of rashers of bacon, it makes a good nourishing meal.

½ lb potatoes   1 egg
2 oz breadcrumbs   Fat for frying
Salt to taste

Peel the potatoes and grate them into a bowl, add the bread-crumbs, salt and beaten egg and mix well. Fry your bacon first, dish up and keep warm, leaving the fat in the frying pan. Into the hot fat put tablespoons of the potato mixture and fry on both sides until golden brown – lovely.

Potato cakes

And here's a way to use up those few potatoes that you might have had over from dinnertime.

½ lb mashed potato	2 oz flour
1 oz butter	Dripping for frying

Re-mash the potatoes well along with the butter, sprinkle in the flour and add a little salt if necessary. Tip out on the floured board and roll out, lightly and quite thin. Cut into rounds with a saucer and fry in very hot fat for about 5 minutes, turning once. Eat at once while piping hot.

Everybody in the village seems to have plenty of apples this season. We love apple dumplings, especially stuffed with a few blackberries.

Baked apple dumplings

Shortcrust pastry (see method page 163)	Sugar
	A few blackberries
4 good sized cooking apples	

First of all make up your shortcrust pastry, according to the size of the family, because each person should have a dumpling. I use 8 oz self-raising flour to 4 oz margarine, 1 oz lard rubbed in and 1 egg to mix; made this way it's nice and short.

Roll out your pastry and cut into four 8″ rounds (use a plate for this). Peel and core the apples and place one on each pastry round. Fill up the centre of the apple with sugar and blackberries. Damp the edges of the pastry, gather it up together round the apple and press to seal the edges. Now turn the dumpling completely over, so that the join is underneath. Make 3 more in the same way. Put the dumplings on to a greased baking sheet, brush the pastry over with a little milk, and put into a hot oven (Gas 7, 425°F) for about 20 minutes, then turn the heat down to Gas 3, 335°F for about another 20 minutes, until the pastry is a nice golden brown and the apple well cooked. Take from the oven, sprinkle with caster sugar and serve either with cream or custard.

The dumplings can be stuffed with mixed dried fruit, brown sugar and a little cinnamon, and honey and raisins makes a nice change too.

Mrs Harvey likes to do things in style and the other day she held a coffee morning in aid of her pet charity. Well, I'd never been into the Harvey home, so I asked Mr Woolley if he would mind if I closed the shop for about three quarters of an hour the other Wednesday because I wanted to go. He hummed and ah'd a bit but when I told him that as far as I knew most everyone in the village was going then he said all right but not to be gone very long. I put the 'closed' sign up at about 10.15 and got on my old bike and was up there just in time for the opening. Oh, she'd lots and lots of things for sale, I picked up a nice earthenware casserole for 10p and lots of bits and bobs that will come in handy later on. The coffee was the real thing, you could smell it all over the house. I know she buys coffee beans and grinds them on a machine because she's asked me for them before now. It was nice to sit in her very nice 'lounge' as she called it, sipping that super coffee – with cream too – she couldn't have made much profit out of that 10p a cup, served with lovely ginger biscuits as well, and I was soon asking whoever had made them, they had a sort of oaty taste. And it seems that Peggy had made them for her, so before I left I made it my business to ask for the recipe, and here it is.

Peggy's ginger biscuits

1 tablespoon golden syrup
4 oz caster sugar
4 oz margarine
4 oz porridge oats
4 oz plain flour

1 dessertspoon ground ginger
1 teaspoon bicarbonate of soda
1 dessertspoon water

Put the syrup, sugar and margarine into a saucepan and melt, but do not boil. Into a mixing bowl put the oats, flour, ginger and bicarb and mix well, then add the contents of the saucepan and lastly the water and mix again. Grease a baking sheet and drop the mixture on to it in small heaps, not too close to each other because the biscuits will spread flat when baked. Cook for about 12 minutes in a pre-heated oven (Gas 3, 335°F) until a nice golden brown. Leave for a few moments before lifting the biscuits off and then cool them on a wire tray to crisp up and get cold. Store in an airtight tin.

Peggy's coconut slices

Peggy had also made some rather nice coconut slices, which she had packed up into half-dozens, so I bought a packet and they were ever so nice too. The recipe is a bit different to the one that I normally use.

Shortcrust pastry
8 oz self-raising flour
4 oz margarine, 1 oz lard
   (rubbed in)
1 egg to mix
Pinch of salt

Coconut topping
5 oz desiccated coconut
2 egg whites
4 oz caster sugar
1 tablespoon plain flour
3 tablespoons raspberry jam

Make the pastry and roll out quite thinly to an oblong shape. Grease a swiss roll tin, line it with the pastry and spread the jam over it. Now whisk up the egg whites until they are very stiff, and then add the coconut, sugar and flour. Spread this mixture evenly over the jam. Bake in a pre-heated oven (Gas 5, 380°F) for about 30 minutes, when the top should be a nice golden brown. Cut into slices while hot but don't remove from the tin until quite cold.

Another gingerbread

Mrs Laura Archer did quite well at the produce show too. She's never been one to do a lot of cooking, so I was pleased to see that she took first prize for her gingerbread. It was a set recipe, we were each given a leaflet so we all stood the same chance, and I must admit Mrs Laura's did look nice.

1 lb self-raising flour
Handful of sultanas
1½ teaspoons ground ginger
A pinch of bicarbonate of
   soda
A few pieces preserved ginger

6 oz margarine
6 oz golden syrup
8 oz soft brown sugar
1 egg
¼ pint milk

Mix all the dry ingredients together except the preserved ginger. Put the margarine, sugar, and syrup into a saucepan and warm gently. Beat up the egg and milk together. Tip the contents of the saucepan into the dry ingredients and add the egg and milk. Line a cake tin with greaseproof paper and put the mixture in. Dot the top with pieces of preserved ginger. Put in a pre-heated oven (Gas 3, 335°F) and cook for about 1½ hours. Leave to cool. Store in an airtight tin, but first wrap the gingerbread in foil. Of course this is a very different type of gingerbread to the one I usually make (see page 149 for my recipe). Where this one is a light golden colour, mine is a rich dark brown.

When I saw Mrs Laura Archer I congratulated her on winning with her lovely gingerbread. 'Thanks, Martha,' she said, 'I know I put a few noses out of joint by winning, you can always tell when folks are upset, they just don't say anything. One thing about you,' she went on, 'you do give folk a bit of credit for what they do and that's more than can be said of a lot of people I know. I'll tell you what, I'll give you a recipe that was closely guarded for years, Fairley used to make it, and after she left I found it tucked away at the back of a drawer, she never would tell me how she made her special almond, apple and date cake. I'll drop it in the very next time I come to the shop, if you promise to bring me a slice the first time you make it.'

Mrs Laura Archer's almond, apple and date cake

6 oz porridge oats	Pinch salt
6 oz margarine	6 oz self-raising flour
4 oz dates, chopped	4 oz brown sugar
1 large cooking apple, peeled and chopped	½ oz flaked almonds
1 level teaspoon baking powder	2 eggs
	1½ tablespoons milk

Put 5½ oz of the oats into a mixing bowl and rub in the margarine. Add the chopped dates, the peeled chopped apple and the baking powder, salt, flour, brown sugar and half the flaked almonds. Beat the eggs and milk together and add this to the mixture stirring well. Put into a well lined cake tin and smooth the top of the cake mixture and sprinkle on the rest of the almonds and the ½ oz of oats. Put into a pre-heated oven (Gas 4, 355°F) for about 1¼ hours.

Well, soon after Mrs Laura Archer had given me the recipe I made the cake and it certainly is nice and very different to any other that I've tasted. Of course, I kept my word and gave her a nice big wedge of it and she reckoned it was just as good as when Fairley used to make it.

My goodness, I've sold that much vinegar the past few weeks, I should think that everybody in the village has been making one sort of pickle or another. It's funny how some people stick to the old ways. Years ago a housewife wasn't able to buy her vinegar already spiced, she bought just ordinary vinegar and a carton of mixed pickling spice, boiled it up together, let it cool and then used it for pickling onions, beetroot, cabbage, eggs and when you made your chutney. Nowadays you can buy vinegar already spiced and this year the price was just the same as the plain vinegar. But the older housewives still religiously buy pickling spice and plain vinegar and spice their own.

This apple chutney is a good tried and tested one. Mrs

Doris Archer told me it's one that belonged to Dan's mother, and that she, Doris, has passed it on to Christine, Jill, Peggy and even on to the next generation – Jennifer and Lilian and of course, Tony's wife Pat. So I think it could be rightly called

The Archers' apple chutney

5 lb apples	½ pint water
1 lb onions	½ lb sultanas
1 heaped teaspoon salt	1 tablespoon mixed pickling
4 level teaspoons dry mustard	spice tied up in muslin
1 level teaspoon ground	¾ pint vinegar
ginger	1½ lb demerara sugar

Peel and chop the apples and onions quite finely. Put them in a saucepan along with the salt, mustard, ginger, water and sultanas, and then drop in the bag of pickling spices. Bring this all up to the boil, stirring well, and simmer for ¾ hour. Now add the vinegar and the sugar and simmer again for at least 1½ hours; by now the chutney will be about as thick as a jam would be. Remove the bag of pickling spices. Put the chutney into dry warm jars and tie down when cold. This should make about 5 lb.

Mrs Mead's blackberry and apple jelly

Polly came into the shop today for some more sugar. She and Sid and Lucy had spent all Sunday afternoon backberrying and she had been so busy making apple and blackberry jelly. Lucy loves it – I expect it's something to do with the fact that she and her mummy and daddy picked them. Anyhow it's good and nourishing for her. Polly said that her mother had told her how to make it, but I think it's a well-known recipe anyway.

Cooking apples   Water and sugar
Blackberries

Wash but don't peel the apples, cut them up quite roughly and place in a large saucepan and half cover with water. Bring to the boil and then simmer until the apples are quite mushy. Then strain this through a piece of muslin or nylon curtaining; tie this up and let it drip into a bowl until all the liquid is out, but *don't squeeze*. In another saucepan put your blackberries and again half cover them with water and stew gently until the fruit is soft. Strain and let drip like the apples. Take the apple juice, mix it with the blackberry juice and measure it. To each pint of liquid add a pound of sugar. Place this in a saucepan, bring to the boil and simmer gently for about 20 minutes. Try the saucer test to see if it sets. When it does pour into warm jars and put the little wax discs on, but don't put the cellophane top on until the jelly is quite cold.

Blackberry wine

Well, I had a first for my raspberry preserve and bottled victorias at the produce show, and tied with Walter for first place for my carrot wine. And my Joby swept the board with his vegetables. He put it all down to the fact that he had a good load of pig manure delivered early in the year. But of course nobody gets good results with anything unless they put a darned lot of hard work into it.

I don't know when I've seen so many blackberries as there are this time. So I've made some blackberry preserve, just like the raspberry (page 132), it looks and tastes lovely and I don't see why it shouldn't keep just as well.

And of course this month its got to be blackberry wine. They make a lovely rich, ruby coloured wine too. If you like yours dry, then don't use quite so much sugar, say three pounds instead of the four that I use, but then we like sweet wine.

3 lb blackberries	4 lb sugar
1 gallon boiling water	½ oz yeast

Wipe the fruit clean, by rolling in a tea towel. Put them into a large bowl and cover with the gallon of boiling water. Allow to stand for 2 days (stirring well twice a day). Strain through muslin and tip the juice back into the bowl. Stir in the sugar until it's dissolved and add the yeast. Cover with thick cloth and leave for 4 days. Pour into a demijohn, fix the airlock and leave until all fermentation has stopped. Then bottle off and the wine will be ready to drink in 6 months.

I always think of October as a cleaning and tidying-up month. There's such a lot to do in the garden. I've been so busy trying to get the wallflower plants in. They – like spring cabbage – really should have been planted by Michaelmas, to give them time to get nicely settled before the cold weather starts, but I just didn't have time to get them in before. Still, they must take their chance with the rest of the plants. We let some of our sweet williams go to seed in the summer-time and now there are young plants all over the garden. I do love the smell of sweet williams and gilly flowers (the country name for wallflowers).

Well, we folk in Ambridge celebrated Harvest Festival early this month. I should think nearly every household in Ambridge had taken something to help decorate the church for this wonderful thanksgiving service. It was a grand sight to see the people streaming into church with their arms full of fruit and vegetables – earthy beetroots, giant marrows and colourful autumn flowers. The church looked so beautiful and bountiful, we really had something to sing thanks for I can tell you. Then the following day we had our harvest supper, and what a wonderful time we had. The tables were bowed down with the food, the housewives of Ambridge had really done us proud, and didn't we do some recipe swapping too!

One lovely surprise there was hot spare ribs. Jill Archer had cooked them and they worked out two each for everybody that went. She had the handling of the tickets so she knew just how many to cater for. She dished up everybody's portion on a plate and put a spoonful of her home-made dip on as well. We ate them with our fingers along with thick crusty, home-made bread and they were lovely. They are so easy to cook it's unbelievable.

Jill Archer's spare ribs and spicy dip

First of all divide the ribs up singly, allowing a couple of ribs for each person. Salt and pepper them well and lay them in a baking dish. Add one or two knobs of dripping and half a cup of water. Cover the dish with foil and bake in a slowish oven (Gas 3, 335°F) for about 2–3 hours, turning the ribs twice during cooking.

Meanwhile make a tasty sauce:

For the dip

1 cup vinegar	1 teaspoon salt
2 tablespoons Worcester sauce	1 teaspoon dry mustard
1 medium onion, sliced finely and fried until transparent	½ cup tomato sauce or ketchup
1 tablespoon sugar	

Mix all the ingredients together and cook gently for 10 minutes. Cool.

Tipperary Irish stew

But the next day it was back to everyday food again, and Nora rushing into the shop just before I shut for dinner to ask for meat cubes. She was going to put an Irish stew in the oven ready for their tea that evening and she said 'Irish stew is nothing without a couple of meat cubes.' I don't entirely agree with her, but willingly served her with the meat cubes. She calls this Tipperary Irish stew and it's got a suet crust on the top.

1 lb stewing beef
1 tablespoon flour
Salt and pepper
2 carrots
2 turnips
2 good sized onions

2 meat cubes
1 pint water
1 teaspoon each thyme and parsley
4 good sized potatoes

Suet crust for top
¼ lb self-raising flour
2 oz suet

Pinch salt
A few drops of water to mix.

First of all cut up the meat into small cubes. Put the salt, pepper and 1 tablespoon of flour on a plate, dip each piece of meat in this before putting it into a good sized casserole. Peel and slice the carrots and turnips and put on top of the meat, now add the meat cubes, water and herbs, put on the lid and cook for 1½ hours in a slowish oven (Gas 3, 335°F). Peel and slice the potatoes and add these to the stew and return to the oven for another 20 minutes.

While this is cooking, make up the suet crust by mixing the flour, suet, salt and water together to make a stiffish paste. Take the lid off the stew, and replace it with the lid-like suet crust. Put back in the oven for a further ½ hour. This is a complete meal – well, except for pudding (sweet).

Pork and onion dish

4 nice pork chops	1 oz breadcrumbs
2 lb onions	Salt and pepper
½ pint water	2 oz butter
1 egg, beaten	

Peel the onions and chop them up quite fine, put them in a saucepan and cover with the ½ pint water and simmer them until they are soft and have used up all the water, when they should be a nice creamy colour. While they are cooking prepare the chops ready for frying. First dip them in the beaten egg and then into the breadcrumbs, adding the salt and pepper to taste. Then fry them in the butter until nicely browned and cooked through. Serve with the onions and creamy mashed potatoes.

Veal cutlets with orange

If you like veal, you will enjoy this way of cooking cutlets. Mind you I only squeeze the orange juice over mine, Joby don't like that sort of thing on his meat.

3 veal cutlets	1 oz breadcrumbs
Salt and pepper	2 oz butter
1 egg, beaten	A little orange juice
1 oz grated cheese	(optional)

Pepper and salt each cutlet, and dip each one in the egg, then in the cheese and breadcrumbs. Fry in the butter until golden brown on both sides. Squeeze the orange juice over before serving.

It's Mrs Dan Archer's birthday this month and Phil's wife Jill invited Dan and Doris up to Brookfield for an evening meal on the great day. Of course, Shula is a great help on these occasions, now that she is really interested in cooking and it was Shula who actually made the main dish which she called Jubilee chicken. Doris told me all about it the next day when she came into the shop for a few things. She was so proud of her grand-daughter, she just had to tell somebody.

'Oh, Martha,' she cried, 'you should have been there, the food looked so lovely laid out. Jill had got out all her best table linen, but it was young Shula who had prepared almost all the food. To tell you the truth I was so overcome I had a little cry. And I think Dan had a lump in his throat too. 'Oh dear,' she went on, 'you worry over the youngsters wondering how they will turn out and really there's no need. Well, after we'd had the meal I asked young Shula how this special chicken in curry sauce was made.

' "Oh Gran," she said, "it's far too complicated for you."

'Never mind about being complicated I told her, I'd like to know what went into it because it was absolutely wonderful. So then she wrote the recipe out. Perhaps you'd like to have a look at it,' she said to me. And Shula was right, it *is* complicated, but all right for anybody who's got the time and patience to do it.

Shula's Jubilee chicken

2 young roasting chickens
3 carrots
Bouquet garni (made up of a sprig each of marjoram, thyme and parsley)
Salt to taste
3–4 peppercorns
Water and a little wine

Poach the chickens along with the carrots, bouquet garni, salt, peppercorns, in water and a little wine – enough to cover – for about 40 minutes, or until tender. Allow to cool in liquid. Joint birds and remove bones carefully.

The curry sauce

1 tablespoon oil
2 oz finely chopped onion
1 dessertspoon curry powder
1 good teaspoon tomato purée
1 wineglass red wine (about ¼ pint or a little more)
1 bay leaf
¼ teaspoon salt
2 teaspoons sugar
Touch of pepper
Slice or 2 of lemon and a teaspoon of lemon juice
¾ pint mayonnaise
1–2 tablespoons apricot purée (apricot jam can be used instead)
3 tablespoons lightly whipped cream
A little extra whipped cream

Heat oil, add onion and cook gently for 3–4 minutes. Add curry powder and cook for about 2 minutes. Now add the tomato purée, wine and bay leaf. Bring to boil, add salt, sugar, pepper, lemon and lemon juice. *Simmer* with pan uncovered for 5–10 minutes. *Strain and cool.* Add bit by bit to the mayonnaise, with apricot purée to taste. Finish with the whipped cream. Take a small amount of sauce – enough to coat chicken – mix with the extra cream and season. Mix chicken and sauce together and arrange on a dish; coat with the extra sauce and decorate with apricot halves and cucumber if you wish. Mrs Archer said they ate theirs with a rice salad which was made up of cooked rice, peas and chopped herbs all mixed in French salad dressing.

Here's an apple pie with a difference. Young Betty Tucker says her mother never made just an *apple* pie, but added currants and mixed peel to hers. I think that this is one of those regional dishes, for I'd never heard of it before.

Betty Tucker's apple pie

For shortcrust pastry
8 oz self-raising flour
5 oz margarine, or margarine and lard
2 teaspoons caster sugar
1 egg

For the filling
2 lb cooking apples, sliced
4 oz currants
2 oz mixed cut peel
$\frac{1}{4}$ teaspoon ground ginger *or* cinnamon
Sugar to taste

Rub the fat into the flour. Add sugar and egg and a little water if necessary. Flour a board and roll the pastry out. Into a good sized pie dish put a layer of apples, sprinkle them with currants and mixed peel, ginger (or cinnamon) and sugar. Repeat until the dish is full. Place a pie funnel in the centre. Cut strips of pastry and place round dampened rim of pie dish then completely cover top with a good layer of pastry. Crimp the edges. Brush with milk or egg white. Bake in a hot oven for about 20 minutes until pastry is golden colour. You can make this on a plate instead of pie dish using just the same method. (If the cooking apples are very hard they may need cooking beforehand.)

Baked egg custard

If we have, say, a nice thick stew and dumplings, I like to make a light pudding to sort of balance things up a bit. And that's when I make an egg custard, mind you my Joby likes a spoonful of jam or jelly to eat with his.

1 pint milk	1 oz caster sugar
3 eggs	Nutmeg

Warm the milk gently in a saucepan. Whisk the eggs and sugar together and add to the warm milk. Pour this into a pie dish and sprinkle over a little grated nutmeg. Now place the pie dish in a deep roasting tin and fill up with water so that it comes halfway up the outside of the pie dish. This is to slow down the cooking and stops the pudding from curdling. Put into a warm oven (Gas 3, 335°F) for about 45 minutes.

Mrs Perkins's honey cakes

Walter came in today and brought me the last pot of his honey, at least for this year. Mind you, he had just taken one to Mrs P. as well, otherwise the fat would be in the fire if she found out I'd had one and she hadn't. I like to keep a jar or two of honey by me, it's handy if you get a cold. Just put a good tablespoon of honey in a cup or glass, add the juice of a lemon and top it with hot water. Drink that down just before you go to bed and that cold will either be gone or you will be feeling very much better come the morning. Of course you can use honey in cooking too, and Mrs P. often makes some honey cakes. Walter's very partial to Mrs P.'s honey cakes I can tell you.

3 oz margarine	1 teaspoon baking powder
6 tablespoons honey	Good pinch salt
3 eggs	4 oz raisins
6 oz plain flour	2 oz chopped nuts (hazel)

Cream margarine and honey together and beat in the eggs one at a time. Fold in the flour, baking powder and salt, then add raisins and nuts. Grease a baking (9" × 12") tin, spread mixture in tin and bake in the oven (Gas 4, 355°F) for about 30 minutes until golden brown. Leave in the tin to cool and cut into bars. These keep very well if you store them in an airtight tin.

Chocolate crispies

There was that much food at the harvest supper, some of it wasn't even started. So the next day the vicar and his wife and Jill Archer made up some nice food parcels and took them round to the older folk in the village who couldn't manage to get to the supper.

But there was one thing that was soon cleared up and that was a sweet crunchy thing that young Pat Archer had made. She called them chocolate crispies and she said that they used to make them a lot in Wales. I certainly hadn't tasted any before, and neither had anyone else I should think, judging by the way they were whipped off the plates. And here's how to make them.

2 oz butter	2 oz chopped walnuts
2 oz caster sugar	2 oz Rice Crispies or
4 oz chopped dates	Special K
1 tablespoon chopped glacé cherries	4 oz cooking chocolate

Melt butter and sugar in saucepan. Remove from heat and add the chopped dates. Bring to boiling point and stir until all is a soft pulp. Take off from heat and stir in cherries, walnuts and crispies. Mix well. Spread out in a (greased) shallow baking tin $\frac{1}{2}$–$\frac{3}{4}$" thick, and press down firmly. Leave to get cold. Melt the chocolate in a basin stood over a saucepan of hot water and when it's nice and runny spread it over the mixture. Cut in squares when the chocolate is set.

Pat Archer says for a change you can put chopped crystallized ginger or coconut in them.

Viennese whirls

It's funny how the seasons change people's eating and drinking habits. A few weeks ago I couldn't keep up with the demand for bottles of squash and ice cream, now it's stuff to make soups with and cough sweets and pies and things. Jethro came in today for 'some a they hot sweets what varnear burns a hole in yer tongue' and he went on, 'My Lizzie said if I was poppin' in yer to ask if you had some vanilla essence tackle, our Clarrie's going to have a go at makin' some fancy cakes what her calls Viennese whirls, I tells her I don't want none of her fancy cakes, I like the old fashioned sort what my Lizzie makes, but I suppose I shall have to try um.'

And Jethro asking for vanilla essence reminded me that I hadn't made any Viennese whirls for ages, my Joby loves them, they're so nice and short and simply melt in your mouth.

$\frac{1}{2}$ lb butter	2 drops vanilla essence
3 oz caster sugar	Pinch salt
$\frac{1}{2}$ lb plain flour	

Beat the butter and sugar together until they are nice and creamy, then mix in the flour a little at a time, adding the essence and salt last. Put the mixture into a piping bag fixed with the biggest star nozzle. Place paper cake cases in a bun tin and squeeze enough mixture in to part fill each case. Now press your forefinger very lightly in the centre of each uncooked cake and drop a very small amount of apricot jam in. Cook in a moderate oven (Gas, 4 355°F) on the second from the top shelf for about 15 minutes.

It was such a good season for tomatoes this year, but we were left with quite a lot of green ones, and what we do at the end of the season is line a cardboard box with plenty of newspaper and place the green tomatoes in it, covering them over well with more newspaper, and do you know within a few days half a dozen or so will have ripened. But I always use up quite a few of the green ones when I make my chutney, and this is how I make it.

Green tomato chutney

3 lb green tomatoes	1 teaspoon cayenne pepper
1 lb onions	$\frac{1}{2}$ teaspoon ground ginger
A handful of salt	$\frac{1}{2}$ lb chopped raisins
2 lb cooking apples	1 lb sugar
1 pint vinegar	

Slice tomatoes and onions very thin and place them on a large dish, sprinkle them with salt and leave for 12 hours. Then drain well. Now peel and slice apples and place in a large saucepan along with all the other ingredients and bring to the boil. Simmer gently for 2 to 3 hours, stirring often with a wooden spoon until the chutney has reached a jam-like consistency. Put into warm jars and tie down with grease-proof or brown paper. This chutney can be eaten straight away, but of course improves if kept a while.

Crab-apple jelly

Young Neil called in the other evening with a bag of crabs for me. He knows that I like to make some crab jelly *and* that I like nice bright red crabs for it. He said when he was doing a bit of hedging the day before he noticed this tree loaded with them, so he took a bag to work the next day to pick some for me. That was a nice thought coming from a youngster I reckon. Mind you, he knows that I'll give him a jar or two. I've asked him to get me some more if he can – so that I can make some crab-apple wine.

Crab apples   Sugar

Remove stalks from the crab apples. Wash them well and cut into quarters, without peeling or coring. Put them into a large saucepan, cover with cold water and bring to the boil slowly. Simmer for about 1½ hours or until the fruit is pulpy. Strain through muslin curtain or a jelly bag, and leave to drip overnight into a bowl. Measure the juice and put into a saucepan. Add 1 lb sugar to each pint of crab juice. Stir while the sugar is dissolving, then bring up to boil and continue to boil briskly for about 10 minutes, then test to see if the jelly will set. Pour into warm clean jars and cover as for jam with waxed and cellophane paper. Some people add 1 or 2 cloves while cooking the crabs, this gives the jelly a lovely flavour, and a friend of mine flavours hers with a couple of scented geranium leaves.

Joby's mum's crab-apple wine

12 lb crab apples   Demerara sugar
1 gallon boiling water   Yeast

Wash the crab apples and cut them in half. Place them in a
good sized crock and pour the gallon of boiling water over
them. Cover the crock and leave for about 5 days, stirring
daily, pressing the crab apples against the side of the crock
at the same time. Then strain off the liquid and to every
gallon of this stir in 3 lb sugar. Keep stirring until all sugar
has dissolved. Now sprinkle the yeast on and cover again for
another week. Strain again, pour the wine into a demijohn,
fix the airlock and leave until the wine has finished working
and then bottle off.

Sloe wine

During this month the sloes show up in the hedgerows,
because the leaves have already dropped off leaving the blue-
black berries for all to see. These make beautiful wine and,
of course, sloe gin, but that's rather expensive.

3 lb sloes   Sugar
1 gallon boiling water   Yeast

Pick off any stalks from the sloes and roll them in a tea towel
to get rid of any dust or dirt. Place the sloes in a good sized
crock or plastic bucket and pour the boiling water over them.
Cover and leave for 4–5 days, stirring daily and crushing the
sloes against the side of the container to help soften the fruit
and to get as much juice out as you can. Then strain the
sloes, measure the juice, and to each gallon add 4 lb sugar.
Stir well until the sugar has dissolved, add the yeast and
cover closely for a week. Pour into your demijohn, fix the air

lock and leave the wine to finish working. When you are ready to bottle off the wine, add two wineglasses of brandy to it. Try and keep the wine for at least a year.

Sloe gin

1 lb sloes   1 pint gin
3 oz caster sugar

Pick off any stalks from the sloes and wipe them by rolling them in a clean tea towel. Have a kilner jar handy, prick each sloe a couple of times with a darning needle and drop them into the jar. Sprinkle on the caster sugar and pour on the gin. Put the top on the jar and screw it up. Gently shake the jar at least once a day for 3 weeks. Then strain off the sloe juiced-gin through fine muslin. Bottle and cork and try to keep for 6 months.

Some folk just put the sloes and sugar in a jar and add the gin after a couple of weeks. But whichever way you make it, you'll find it very potent stuff.

NOVEMBER

November is about the only month of the year that I'm glad
to see the back of. I don't mind the cold, hard weather of
winter, it's the damp dark days that we usually get in
November that gets me, and I simply can't abide fog. And
the days seem so short, too. Even so there's quite a bit of
colour in the hedgerow along the lane, bright red hips, pinky
orange spindleberries with the grey old man's beard (Travel-
ler's Joy) climbing all over the place. But even the dullest
month has its compensations. At least it's too cold and dark
to do anything more in the evenings than just sit by a great
big log fire. Joby has got a big stack of ash and oak logs
just outside our back door so we don't have to go far to get
them. The sugar beet harvest is over at last, and Jethro is
glad about this, he's been coming into the shop plastered
with mud. 'I wish you sold hot pies, Martha,' Jethro remarked the other day, 'I know the pub do but everytime I
goes in thur fer one I 'as to 'ave a drink as well, not that I be
complaining about that really, but that beer do seem a bit
cold midday.'

Well, bonfire night is over for another year, it amazes me
the money folk spend on fireworks; still the children enjoy
them, so do some of the grown-ups too, by all acounts. Polly
said she didn't know who was most excited at their little
bonfire party, Sid or Lucy.

Well, this is the time for plenty of soups and stews and here's a good way of cooking an old hen that's finished laying and making two meals from it. The first is called

Cockie leekie

1 old hen	Salt and pepper to taste
2 tablespoons vinegar	4 or 5 prunes (stewed)
½ cup rice	1 tablespoon chopped
4 leeks, sliced	parsley

Pluck the bird and clean out the inside, saving the liver, gizzard and heart. Put the vinegar and about a quart of water into a bowl and leave the bird to soak in this overnight. Next morning place the hen in a large saucepan, along with the liver, gizzard and heart, cover with water and simmer over a steady heat for about 2½ hours. Now add the rice and sliced leeks and salt and pepper to taste and simmer again until the leeks are cooked. Add the prunes which have been stewed and stoned (do not add the juice). Sprinkle on the parsley. Take out the hen and cut off all the breast meat and put this back into the soup, and simmer for a few minutes. Now the soup is ready to serve.

A good tasty soup

And here's how to make another meal with the rest of the bird: The old bird will be fairly tender after the cooking in the last recipe, so cut it up, taking off all the meat. Put this into a saucepan along with the bones and carcass. Then lightly fry a couple of peeled, sliced onions, two or three peeled, sliced carrots and a leek or two, and add these to the meat and bones and cover with water and simmer for about an hour. Then add a teaspoon each of chopped parsley, thyme and marjoram and pepper and salt to taste. In a separate basin put a table-spoon of plain cornflour and mix it with about a quarter of a pint of milk, making it into a smooth paste. Tip this into the saucepan and bring almost up to the boil. Then lift out all the bones and soup will be ready to serve.

Mrs Laura Archer is quite surprising really, she's always making out that she's not interested in cooking and yet, in just ordinary conversation in the shop, she comes out with some really unusual ideas. Take the other day. Young Christine Johnson was saying that they were going to have some pork fillet for their tea, and her aunt Laura turned round and asked her how she was going to cook it. 'Well just fry it in some fat as I've always done,' she replied.

'Ah,' Mrs. Laura said, 'you should try cooking like they do in New Zealand with parsley and caraway seeds.' Well, as she was telling young Christine the method, I was busy scribbling it down, and the next time we had pork fillet (some folk call it tenderloin) I tried it out on my Joby. He didn't care for the caraway seeds in it, so if you are not partial to them they could be left out. But cooked this way the meat simply melted in your mouth and it was ever so tasty.

Mrs Laura Archer's pork fillet

2 lb pork fillet (or tenderloin)
Salt and pepper to taste
1 good pinch caraway seeds (optional)

1 good sized onion
1 oz butter
1 tablespoon chopped parsley

First remove any skin from the meat and lay it in a piece of cooking foil, and season it well with pepper and salt and the caraway seeds. Now peel and chop the onion and fry it for a few minutes in a frying pan with the butter and finely chopped parsley. Tip this on to the top of the pork fillet and then fold the cooking foil up so as to make a neat parcel of the meat. Lay this in a meat tin and bake in a moderate oven (Gas 4, 355°F) for about an hour. Then fold back the foil and cook for a further 7–8 minutes to brown up the meat. Lovely with creamy mashed poatoes and peas.

Mary Pound's beef skirt and dumplings

1 lb beef skirt
¼ lb kidney
1 tablespoon flour
Pepper and salt

A little dripping
1 onion, sliced
Water and 2 meat cubes

Dumplings
¼ lb flour
2 oz suet

Pinch salt
Little water to mix

Cut up the beef and kidney and dip it in the seasoned flour and fry lightly in the dripping for a few minutes. Put into a casserole. Now fry the sliced onion and add this to the meat. Cover with water and sprinkle on the meat cubes. Cover and cook in a slow oven (Gas 3, 335°F) for about 3 hours. Mix together the ingredients for the dumplings, add them to the casserole and cook for a further ½ hour.

George Barford brought me a lovely sandy hare the other day. There had been a shoot on the estate and the men had been given a couple each. 'Nora don't care for them,' he said, handing me the animal which he had carefully gutted. 'She reckons they're too strong,' he went on, 'but I know that you and Joby like um.'

'Like um,' I cried, 'we loves um, ah that'll do us for two or three days.' And this is how Joby's mum used to cook um.

Joby's mum's hare

1 hare (you can find out how to skin one at the beginning of the recipe for leveret casserole on page 141)
1 tablespoon flour
Pepper and salt
A bunch of herbs (parsley, thyme and marjoram)
2 or 3 onions, each stuck with a clove (optional)
Slice of lemon peel
½ lb streaky bacon
2 tablespoons tomato ketchup
A drop of port wine
A knob of butter

Cut up the hare into joints and wash in salted water. Dry, and then flour each piece in the well-seasoned tablespoon of flour. Put these into a good sized casserole along with the bunch of herbs, the whole onions, lemon peel and chopped up bacon. Cover with water and place in a slowish oven (Gas 3, 335°F) for about 2½ hours. Mix in any seasoned flour that is left, along with the tomato ketchup, and the port. Add a knob of butter into the paste, add to the casserole and cook for a further 20–30 minutes. Serve with redcurrant jelly.

Partridge casserole

Prue Forrest gave me this recipe, it's a nice tasty dish and one where you can use an old bird.

1 partridge	Cider
4 oz streaky bacon	1 tablespoon flour
1 onion	Salt and pepper to taste
1 pint meat stock	1 oz dripping
2 oz mushrooms (optional)	

After you have picked and drawn your bird, wash it out well and then cut it up into joints. Put the flour, salt and pepper on a plate and dip each joint in it, then fry them in the dripping until they are nice and brown on both sides. Tip into a casserole. Now chop up the bacon and onion and fry them lightly and add them to the casserole. Cover with the stock and about quarter of a pint of cider. Tip in any seasoned flour that might be left on the plate. Also add the mushrooms. Cover and cook in a steady oven (Gas 4, 355°F), for about two hours or until the partridge is cooked. Serve with mashed potatoes, mashed swede and Brussels sprouts.

Braised celery hearts

About 4 heads celery
2 oz dripping
½ pint stock

Salt and pepper
1 tablespoon chopped
parsley

Take off all the outside stalks of the celery (don't throw them
away they will make lovely soup) until you have just the
hearts left. Wash them well in salt water and then drain.
Fry them very gently in the dripping until they are a nice
golden brown. Put the hearts into a saucepan and cover with
the stock and simmer very gently for about 20 minutes. Carefully take the hearts out and keep them warm on a dish. Boil
down the stock until it is about a third of its original quantity.
It should now be quite thick. Season to taste. Pour this over
the hearts and then sprinkle on the parsley. This is lovely
served with a nice meat pudding.

Braised carrots

1 lb carrots
1½ oz butter
Salt and pepper
¼ teaspoon sugar

½ pint brown stock
1 tablespoon chopped
parsley

Peel the carrots and cut lengthways. Put them in a saucepan
of cold water and bring to the boil. Strain. Using the same
pan, melt the butter, toss in the carrots and fry for a few

minutes. Now tip them and any juice into a casserole, add the salt and pepper, sugar and stock; cover and cook gently for about an hour at Gas 3, 335°F. When serving, sprinkle with the chopped parsley.

I always aim to get my Christmas puddings made by about the middle of November. Well, we should really all get them made by 'Stir up Sunday' – the last Sunday after Trinity and the week before the first Sunday in Advent. But of course as very young children we just thought that 'Stir up Sunday' was in fact the proper day to stir up the puddings and have a wish, and we used to chant 'Stir up our Puddings O Lord' as we stirred and of course secretly wished for something special. But on the more serious side, the words in the Collect for the last Sunday after Trinity begin 'Stir up, we beseech thee O Lord, the wills of thy faithful people.'

And this is how I make my Christmas puddings. I read in Joby's mum's recipe book that she used to use flour whereas I use breadcrumbs and no flour at all. And by using breadcrumbs you get a lighter more crumbly pudding which will keep from one Christmas to the next.

Christmas pudding

Into a large mixing bowl put the following, in this order:

¾ lb fine breadcrumbs
½ lb raisins
½ lb currants
½ lb sultanas
½ lb suet
4 oz chopped mixed peel
1 grated carrot
½ lb soft brown sugar
1½ oz blanched almonds,
   finely chopped

½ the juice and grated rind
   of a lemon
½ teaspoon nutmeg
½ teaspoon salt
2 teaspoons mixed spice
4 large eggs
½ pint old beer or stout
   to mix

Stir all the ingredients together well and if it's not quite wet enough add a little milk. Put the mixture into well greased basins and tie them down with greaseproof and foil paper. Boil for 6–8 hours. Take off covers and allow puddings to dry out well before covering with clean, dry paper. Store in a cool place and boil for a further 2 hours on the day that you eat them.

Rum butter

Here's how to make rum butter to eat with the Christmas pudding, but it can also be used as a filling for a spongecake, and I like it spread on nice thin bread.

½ lb soft brown sugar
4 oz butter

Little grated nutmeg or
   cinnamon to taste
3 or 4 tablespoons of rum

Cream the butter and sugar together, add the nutmeg or cinnamon and lastly the rum. Beat until you have a nice creamy mixture.

Mrs Doris Archer's mincemeat

I like to get the mincemeat made this month as well, but leave making the cake until about the first week in December.

Mrs Doris Archer gave me this very old recipe for mince-meat and, like the pudding, it will easily keep from one year to the next. If, after keeping a jar or two for a year, you open it and find that the top is a bit dry, just pour a drop of brandy on and stir it in.

1 lb apples
1 lb suet
1 lb raisins
1½ lb currants
½ lb mixed peel
2 lb soft brown sugar
½ oz ground ginger

Pinch salt
2 flat tablspoons nutmeg
½ lb almonds
The rind and juice of four lemons
1 glass brandy
¼ pint raisin wine

Peel and core the apples, chop them finely and put into a large basin. Add the chopped suet (if you buy it in a packet this will already be done), the chopped raisins, currants, peel, sugar, ginger, salt, nutmeg and the blanched chopped almonds (or flaked ones will do) and the rind from the lemons. Now separately mix up the brandy, lemon juice and raisin wine together and pour this over the mincemeat and stir well. Stir again before putting the mincemeat into dry jam jars. Cover in the usual way.

Steamed pudding

There's nothing nicer on a cold winter's day than a lovely' light, steamed pudding, you can make a plain one and then just put a few slices of cooking apple and sugar in the basin first. But of course you can use any sorts of fruit or any sorts of jam, or golden syrup. Or for a change you can use currants, mixed dried fruit or raisins. Here's how to make the basic pudding, then you can use what variations you like. This is enough to fill a pint pudding basin as the mixture will rise.

4 oz self-raising flour
2 oz margarine

2 oz sugar
1 egg and a little milk

Simply rub the margarine and flour together, add the sugar and lastly the egg and a little milk to make quite a soft batter. Grease a pudding basin, put in any of the ingredients that I listed. Pour in the batter and tie down either with grease-proof paper or foil. Half fill a saucepan with boiling water and slip the basin in, don't let the water come over the top of the basin. Bring to the boil and keep the pudding boiling for 1–1½ hours, adding more water as it boils away.

Joby's favourite steamed pudding is a ginger one, so to the basic recipe I add 1 teaspoon of ground ginger and in the bottom of the basin I put 2 good tablespoons of golden syrup. Lovely!

Mrs Perkins's date and apple cake

I saw Mrs Perkins standing by her front door the other day and she insisted that I should go in for a few minutes. She's got a nice cosy home in her council bungalow and it was nice to sit by the fire and chat for a little while. 'Course we had to have a cup of tea and she had made a date and apple cake; lovely and moist it was, and went down a treat after a busy day in the shop. She said that she had got the recipe out of a magazine at some time.

6 oz self-raising flour	1 large cooking apple
2 oz margarine	1 egg
3 oz caster sugar	About 2½ tablespoons milk
2 oz chopped dates	

Put the flour and margarine into a mixing bowl and rub up with the fingers till it looks like breadcrumbs. Add the caster sugar and the dates. Peel and core the apple and cut half of it into slices, put these on one side, but mix the rest, chopped up fine with the flour etc. Beat up the egg and milk together and add this to make all into a nice stiffish dough. Line a loaf tin with greaseproof paper and pour in the mixture, then lay the slices of apple on to the top of the loaf. Put into a pre-heated oven (Gas 5, 380°F) for about 1¼ hours. Turn out and cool on a rack. Don't cut the loaf until it's quite cold. Lovely spread with butter, or eaten just as it is.

Peggy's rich chocolate cake

Mrs P. also told me about a super chocolate cake that her daughter Peggy makes for her sometimes. 'Peg knows that I likes to always have a bit of cake in the tin to offer visitors', Mrs P. said, 'and she knows as how Mr Gabriel's very partial to a slice of her chocolate cake, strikes me that's all he comes in for, to see what he can cadge.'

6 oz self-raising flour	4 oz golden syrup
2 oz cocoa	4 small eggs
8 oz margarine	1 oz chopped nuts (optional)
4 oz moist dark brown sugar	1 rounded tablespoon granulated sugar

Put flour and cocoa into a bowl. In another bowl cream the margarine and the brown sugar until light and fluffy and then add the syrup. Now beat in the eggs one at a time. Fold in the flour and cocoa and mix well. Add nuts if required. Pour the mixture into a greased 7″ cake tin and bake in the centre of a moderate oven (Gas 3, 335°F) for about an hour. Take the cake out of the oven and sprinkle the top with the tablespoonful of granulated sugar and then cook for a further ½ hour. Leave in the tin to cool for 5 minutes, turn out and cool on rack. This makes a very dark moist cake that will keep well for 2–3 weeks if it's wrapped in foil and kept in a tin

Crisp flapjacks

There are all sorts of different ways of making flapjacks, but I think this is quite the easiest that I've come across.

| 7 oz butter or margarine | 4 oz demerara sugar |
| 8 oz porridge oats | Pinch salt |

First melt the fat and the sugar in a saucepan, then stir in the oats and the salt. Grease a swiss roll type tin and tip the mixture in, flattening it down with the palm of the hand. Bake in a slow oven (Gas 3, 335°F) for about 35 minutes. Mark out into slices while hot and gently ease a knife blade round the sides, but don't remove from the tin until quite cold.

At this time of the year there's not much available to make home-made wines with so if you can cadge a pound of wheat from a farmer really all you've got to buy are the raisins and the sugar, and it makes a wonderful liquor – almost like whisky.

Wheat and raisin wine

1 lb wheat	4 lb sugar
1 lb raisins, chopped	1 gallon water
1 lb old potatoes, peeled and chopped	1 oz yeast

Put the wheat, chopped raisins, potatoes and sugar into a crock or plastic bucket, cover with 1 gallon of *boiled* cold water. Sprinkle the yeast on top and cover with a cloth. Leave for 2 weeks and just give a little stir with a wooden spoon each day. Strain into a demijohn to work for about 3 weeks and then bottle off. This wine will be ready in 6 months.

DECEMBER

Merry Christmas

BIRO

We do get some lovely sunsets during this month. On sharp cold clear evenings the sun goes down like a ball of fire, lighting up the sky and reflecting bright red into the cottage windows till they look almost as if the dwellings themselves are on fire.

I do love to watch a plough cutting through the soil at this time of the year. Young Neil has been busy ploughing in the field just beyond our cottage, and when I rode back to work this afternoon I'll bet there was six dozen or more birds, following behind where the plough had turned up the soil. I could see rooks and crows, peewits (plovers) seagulls all pecking about, no doubt finding some nice choice grubs.

There seems to be plenty of hips and haws about this year and the berries on the holly are thick as bell ropes. We've already had some carol singers, very nice singing it was too. Members of the Ambridge Youth Club which, of course, included Neil, came round the village carol singing and they gave all the money they collected to the blind. When they called on us, we let them sing 'We Three Kings' and then Joby opened the door and asked them all in. About twenty of them there was, they came tumbling into our cottage all bright and gay they looked too. So out came the home-made wine, mind you I took particular notice not to give um anything too strong, and then we handed round some mince pies that I'd just made for ourselves really. Oh they did enjoy them.

It's beginning to look quite Christmassy in the village. Most folks have Christmas trees in their windows, bedecked with coloured lights shining out on the December darkness. The weather has turned quite cold and frosty. Walter came into the shop today and he reckons it's cold enough for snow.

Mr Woolley called in to see if I was managing all right with all the extra work on the post office side. I told him the rush in the grocery trade at Christmas wouldn't start until after people had got all their cards and parcels off, so the work load sort of balances itself out. And there's a lot more folk delivering their own cards this year, at least to their friends in the village. I never did see the sense of posting a card to somebody who you most likely see every day. Young Tony Archer came in for some stamps today and he'd got a most shocking cold. I told him what he wanted was a good big bowl of onion soup before he went to bed, I'll bet that would shake his cold off. So he said that he'd get Pat to make some that night, as he'd tried everything to get rid of it.

Thick onion soup

1 lb onions	2 tablespoons cornflour
A knob of dripping	1 teaspoon dry mustard
Salt and pepper	Water

Melt the fat in a frying pan. Peel and slice the onions finely and cook them gently in the dripping for about 10 minutes, but don't brown them. Add the salt and pepper. In a separate basin mix the cornflour, mustard and a little water together to make a smooth paste. Add this to the onions and stir well. Transfer all from the frying pan into a saucepan and add about a pint of water. Bring the contents almost to the boil and continue to simmer for about 20 minutes. Serve very hot, and go to bed before you start sweating.

Cream of celery soup

This is another good warming soup and it can be made from the outside stalks of celery – you know, the pieces that are too tough to eat raw.

4 or 5 outside celery stalks	Salt and pepper
2 good sized onions	2 tablespoons rice
1 small turnip	2 tablespoons flour
2 pints cold water	1 oz butter
	1 pint milk

Wash the celery and cut it up in small pieces, and put them in a saucepan. Peel and slice the onions and turnip and add them to the celery. Tip in the cold water and add the salt and pepper and bring up to the boil. Now add the rice and boil again for about ½ hour, stirring occasionally. Make a white sauce with the flour, butter and milk, first frying the butter and flour together for a few moments, then add the milk and bring up to the boil so that the sauce is quite thick. Now strain the soup on to the white sauce. Warm up gently but do not let it boil.

At this time of the year, most housewives are a bit pushed for time. Here's a way to make up sausage meat and pastry which will serve the same purpose as sausage rolls, only you don't have to fiddle with making them all separately. It's called sausage plait.

Sausage plait

Puff pastry   1 lb sausage meat

Make up the puff pastry in the usual way (as for the Banbury cakes, page 148). Roll out quite thinly into a long, oblong shape and place it on a baking sheet. Mentally divide your pastry shape into 3. Spread your sausage meat and lay it on the pastry so that it completely fills the centre strip. Now with a sharp knife, starting $\frac{1}{2}''$ from the top of both sides of the uncovered pastry, cut it at $\frac{1}{2}''$ intervals, working outwards from the meat to the end of the shape. Now working from the top, again, fold each strip of pastry, criss-crossing them over each other, over the sausage meat, so as to make a plait-like effect. Brush the pastry over with a little beaten egg and cook in a hot oven (Gas 8, 445°F) for about 20 minutes until golden brown. Leave to cool and cut a slice when needed.

Pork and pigs' kidneys

¾ lb lean pork (this could be
the remains of a joint)
2 pigs' kidneys
Salt and pepper to taste
1 teaspoon chopped sage

½ pint stock or water
2 good sized apples
2 good sized onions
4 big potatoes

Cut up the pork and the kidneys into small pieces and put at the bottom of a pie dish, add the salt and pepper and sage and then add the stock or water. Peel and slice the apples and vegetables and mix them well and pile them on top of the meat. Cover the top of the dish with foil and cook for about 1½ hours at Gas 4, 355°F. Take off the foil and cook for a further ½ hour. With this dish you have plenty of vegetables so it is a meal in itself. But you could serve it with greens or sprouts.

Most turkeys are sold already dressed for the oven which makes things a lot easier for the housewife. Some folk like chestnut stuffing with theirs, while others, like me, prefer the old-fashioned sort made with chopped bacon, onions, breadcrumbs and the turkey liver and herbs, with the neck end stuffed with sausage meat.

Roast turkey with an old-fashioned stuffing

This is how I make my stuffing:

I take about 6 streaky rashers and cut them up small and fry them lightly in a little fat, then I peel and slice 2 good sized onions and fry them for a few minutes. Then chop up the liver and add all this to ½ lb breadcrumbs, add salt and pepper to taste and mix well. Chop up 2 heaped tablespoons of parsley and one of thyme. Mix all together with 1 egg. Stuff the turkey with this and fill the neck end with pork sausage meat.

Fold the wings of the bird behind its shoulders. Press the legs down well and tie with kitchen string. Now wrap the breast and legs with streaky bacon fixing it with wooden cocktail sticks. Cover the bird with plenty of dripping and cook in a pre-heated oven (Gas 5, 380°F). Turkeys need cooking about 15 minutes to the pound.

Here are three different ways to make stuffing for chickens, etc.

Thyme and parsley stuffing

4 oz breadcrumbs	Salt and pepper
1 big onion, grated	1 oz dripping
1 tablespoon chopped parsley	1 egg
1 heaped teaspoon thyme	¼ lb sausage meat

Mix all the ingredients together with the hand.

Sage and onion stuffing

For a sage and onion stuffing just leave out the parsley and thyme and the sausage meat and add 2 teaspoons of fine chopped sage.

Carol Treggoran's chestnut stuffing

1 lb chestnuts	3 or 4 oz breadcrumbs
¼ pint milk	Salt and pepper
2 oz butter	½ lb sausage meat

Prick each chestnut and put them into a saucepan of cold water, bring to the boil and cook for about 12 minutes and leave to cool. Take each nut out and remove the skins. Put them back in a saucepan and add about ¼ pink of milk and simmer until the chestnuts are soft and all the liquid used up. Rub them through a fine sieve. Melt the butter, stir in the breadcrumbs and chestnuts, salt and pepper and then work in the sausage meat mixing all together well. This is specially for the turkey.

This is a super dish according to Jill Archer. She says that she often makes it during the 'game season'. She gave me the recipe, but of course I've never tried it, it would be far too much for Joby and me anyhow. But she reckons that it's very tasty and filling. I should think so too with all that meat.

Jill Archer's game pie

2 pigeons
1 partridge or pheasant
1 rabbit
2 large onions
½ lb carrots
½ lb swedes

½ lb parsnips
1 teaspoon each thyme,
parsley and marjoram
Pepper and salt
½ lb diced stewing beef

Flaky pastry
1 lb plain flour
14 oz lard

Water to mix
Squeeze of lemon

When you have plucked and dressed the birds, and skinned and paunched the rabbit,* wash them well in salt water. Lay all the game in a large casserole along with the peeled sliced vegetables, herbs, salt and pepper. Cover and cook in a warm oven (Gas 3, 335°F) for about 3 hours. Take out the game and remove all the bones (keep these for soup). Now layer the game in a large pie dish also adding the raw beef. Thicken some of the strained liquid with a little plain flour and cover the meat with this. (Keep the cooked vegetables and mix this with the game bones to make soup for the next day.) Place a pie funnel in the centre of the dish and cover with flaky pastry. Bake in a hot oven (Gas 6 or 7, 400–425°F) for 30–40 minutes.

*If you're not sure how to do these two operations turn to page 25 for instructions on how to pluck a bird; page 141 will tell you how to skin a rabbit or hare.

Mrs Adamson the vicar's wife was telling me the other day that one of the vicar's favourite supper dishes is macaroni cheese. 'He never seems to tire of it, Martha,' she said. 'If I don't cook one at least twice a week during the wintertime he'll remind me by saying something like "By the way, dear, did you mention that we are to have macaroni cheese for supper tonight?", and then he smiles knowing darn well that he's just giving me a gentle hint. Anyway,' she went on, 'I'd better take another three quarters of that cheddar cheese, that's a lovely tasty piece you've got this week.' Joby and me like macaroni cheese too, specially for supper on a Saturday night.

Macaroni cheese

3 oz macaroni	Salt and pepper
1 oz butter	1 teaspoon dry mustard
1 oz flour	5 oz grated cheddar cheese
1 pint milk	

Put the macaroni into a saucepan, cover it with boiling water and cook it until it's quite soft. Drain. Make a white sauce with the butter, flour and milk. Put the macaroni into a pie dish and add the salt and pepper, mustard and all but about 1 oz of the grated cheese, pour on the white sauce and then sprinkle the remaining cheese on the top. Place in a hottish oven (Gas 5, 380°F) for about ½ hour when it should be nicely brown on the top.

One thing that'll warm the cockles of your heart during the cold weather is a good spotted dog, or spotted dick as some people call them. Mind you, some of the younger generation don't know what us old uns are on about when we speak of such things. Take the other day when Jethro was in the shop getting his Lizzie some groceries; as he was leaving he said, 'Well, Martha, I be awf home to a gret spotted dog.'

'Ah lovely,' I said, 'just the job this weather, you can't beat um.'

Well, there was a young mum in the shop at the time, definitely not a country girl, and she turned round and give Jethro and me such a funny look. But made with butcher's suet there's nothing so warming as a good suet pudding. And if you can't get butcher's suet then you can make do with a packet.

Spotted dog or spotted dick

8 oz self-raising flour	4 oz currants (more if you
4 oz chopped suet	wish)
2 oz sugar	A little water to mix

Put the flour, suet, sugar and currants into a mixing bowl. Add enough water to make a stiffish dough. Tip out on to a floured board and shape into a roll. *Well flour* a piece of white cloth, lay the pudding on it and roll up into a parcel and sew up the ends of the cloth (the flour will keep water from getting into the pudding). Place the pudding into a saucepan of boiling water and cook for at least 3 hours, adding more water as it boils away. To serve, cut the stitches and unroll the pudding. Let it dry off for a few moments. Lovely eaten in slices hot, sprinkled with sugar, but some folk like a drop of runny custard on theirs. If there is any left the following day, slip a slice in with a rasher of bacon at breakfastime, super!

For a change you can leave out the currants and just serve the pudding plain with hot golden syrup on or your favourite jam.

Joby's mum's bakewell tart

Here's another of Joby's mum's recipes and by the side of this recipe she had written 'only for very special occasions'.

Shortcrust pastry
8 oz flour
4 oz margarine and lard mixed
Pinch of salt
Water to mix

For the filling
Apricot jam
$\frac{1}{4}$ lb sugar
$\frac{1}{4}$ lb butter
3 eggs, well beaten
Almond essence
Whipped cream

Make up the shortcrust pastry. Grease a sandwich tin, line with the pastry and cover the bottom with a good thick layer of apricot jam. In a separate basin put the sugar and butter and cream them together until soft. Then add the well beaten eggs and lastly the almond essence. Spread this mixture over the jam and bake in a pre-heated oven (Gas 5, 380°F) for about 30 minutes. Take from the oven and leave to get cold, then pile whipped cream on the top.

Christmas cake

Well, the first thing I did this month was to bake my Christmas cake.

½ lb butter or margarine
½ lb soft brown sugar
4 eggs, well beaten
A few drops vanilla and almond essence
1 teaspoon grated lemon rind
10 oz plain flour
1 teaspoon each cinnamon *and* mixed spice
1 level teaspoon baking powder
½ lb currants
½ lb sultanas
½ lb raisins
2 oz chopped walnuts *or* almonds (sometimes I put in 2 oz cherries instead of nuts)

Cream butter and sugar, add the well beaten eggs – add essence, lemon rind (I then mix the cinnamon, spice and baking powder into the flour, and *then* add the fruit and nuts – mixing it all up well *before* putting it into the egg, butter and sugar mixture. Now add 1 dessertspoonful of brandy and stir gently until all is well mixed. Well grease and line with several thicknesses of greaseproof paper an 8″ tin and pour the cake mixture in. Make a 1½″ deep well in centre of cake and leave in tin to settle for a few minutes. Then put into a pre-heated oven (Gas 3, 335°F) on the middle shelf and cook for 1 hour, then turn down to Gas 2, 310°F and cook for another 2 hours.

Almond paste

1 whole egg and 1 yolk
8 oz caster sugar
1 teaspoon almond or vanilla essence
8 oz icing sugar
8 oz ground almonds

Whisk the eggs and caster sugar over hot water until blended. Remove from over the hot water and add essence, icing sugar and ground almonds. Now turn on to a board that has been dusted with icing sugar and knead until firm. Leave for 1 hour before using. This is easy to mould and will keep well in a polythene bag.

I put my almond paste on the cake about a week before Christmas. Then two days before the great day I mix up my icing sugar with the white of an egg and a few spots of lemon juice, and simply do a snow scene by roughing up the icing and then put a little fir tree and father Christmas on, and tie on a bright red cake frill.

White icing

8 oz icing sugar   1 tablespoon lemon juice
White(s) of 1 or 2 eggs
   (depending on the size)

Beat together gradually the egg white(s), the icing sugar and the lemon juice.

Shrewsbury biscuits

Most housewives like to make lots of mince pies, biscuits, sweetmeats and things before Christmas and then everybody can sit back and enjoy a few days of lazing about and eating up, or offering to visitors, all the lovely things they made beforehand. Among many other things I like to make a batch of Shrewsbury biscuits for Christmas.

4 oz butter   8 oz plain flour
4 oz caster sugar   A drop of vanilla essence
1 egg

Just cream the butter and sugar together, add the egg, fold in the flour and essence and form into a dough with the hands. Roll out very thinly, cut into rounds and place on baking sheet and cook for about 10 minutes in a moderate oven (Gas 4, 355°F). Take out of the oven, slide the biscuits off with a fish slice and leave to cool on a cake rack.

Rum truffles

About the middle of the month Jill Archer came in with a little box all tied up with pretty paper and handed it to me. 'Here you are, Martha,' she said, 'just a little something for you and Joby to enjoy over Christmas.' Bless her, she had made some rum truffles and they were very moreish, and Joby and me polished them off long before Christmas Day. So the next time she came in I had to admit that we had eaten them, and she said 'Right, if I give you the recipe you can make some yourself for Christmas.' And they really are quite easy to make.

4 oz dark cooking chocolate	2 tablespoons double cream
4 oz icing sugar	2 tablespoons rum
1 egg yolk	Chocolate vermicelli
2 tablespoons ground almonds	

Melt the chocolate over a basin of hot water, beat in the icing sugar, egg yolk, almonds, cream and rum and pound it all together until the mixture is smooth, and form into little balls. Roll each truffle in a little chocolate vermicelli and leave to get quite cold.

Prue's chocolate glacé cherries

We were asked round to Tom and Prue's one evening, just for a drink and a chatter. Mind you it didn't stop at that. Prue had made all sorts of nice things to eat. What took my fancy was some chocolate glacé cherries she had made. She said that when she was helping out at Brookfield she often used to make them for Mrs Phil, not just for Christmas but for any special do.

Glacé cherries
Brandy

Dark cooking chocolate (you could use a slab of dark chocolate if you wished)

Put the cherries to soak overnight in a little brandy. Place the cooking chocolate in a basin over a saucepan of hot water and leave it until it has gone soft. Spear each cherry with a cocktail stick and plunge it into the melted chocolate, covering it, put on a dish and then pull out the stick. Repeat until you have used up all the cherries and chocolate. Leave to set.

WHO'S WHO IN THE ARCHERS' COUNTRY COOKBOOK

Members of The Archers' cast who are mentioned in the book:

Mr Dan Archer, semi-retired farmer

Mrs Doris Archer, wife of Dan Archer

Mrs Jill Archer, Philip Archer's wife – Philip is the son of Dan and Doris Archer

Mrs Laura Archer, sister-in-law of Dan and Doris Archer

Mrs Peggy Archer, daughter-in-law of Dan and Doris Archer

Mr Tony Archer, son of Peggy and the late Jack Archer

Mrs Pat Archer, wife of Tony

Miss Shula Archer, daughter of Phil and Jill Archer

Mrs Dorothy Adamson, vicar's wife

Brian Aldridge, farmer and husband of Jennifer

Mrs Jennifer Aldridge, daughter of Peggy and the late Jack Archer

Gordon Armstrong ⎫
George Barford ⎬ Gamekeepers for Mr Woolley

Mrs Lilian Bellamy, daughter of Peggy and the late Jack Archer

Mr Ralph Bellamy, husband of Lilian Archer

Mrs Blossom, housekeeper to Mr Lucas

Harry Booker, village postman

Neil Carter, works for Phil Archer

Mrs Catermole, lives in Ambridge with a rather large family

Mrs Barbara Drury, policeman's wife

Colin Drury, village policeman

Fairley, used to work for Mrs Laura Archer

Mr Tom Forrest, brother of Doris Archer

Mrs Prue Forrest, wife of Tom

Walter Gabriel, village character
Mrs Jean Harvey, rents Bull Farm
Mrs Christine Johnson, daughter of Dan and Doris Archer
Paul Johnson, husband of Christine
Clarrie Larkin, Jethro's daughter
Jethro Larkin, farm worker on Phil Archer's farm
Lizzie Larkin, wife of Jethro
Nora McAuley, barmaid at The Bull
Mrs Mead, Polly Perks's mother
Mrs Polly Perks, licencee of The Bull
Mr Sid Perks, Polly's husband
Lucy Perks, their small daughter
Mrs Perkins, mother of Peggy Archer and great friend of
    Walter Gabriel
Mrs Mary Pound, farmer's wife
Ken Pound, farmer and husband of Mary
Mrs Carol Treggoran, owner of market garden
Mrs Betty Tucker, wife of Mike Tucker
Mike Tucker, farm worker and husband of Betty
Joby Woodford, forester on the Bellamy estate
Martha Woodford, wife of Joby, runs village shop and Post
    Office
Mr Jack Woolley, owner of Grey Gables Country club, village
    shop, and garden centre

BESTSELLERS FROM ARROW

All these books are available from your bookshop or newsagent or you can order them direct. Just tick the titles you want and complete the form below.

☐	BEAUTIFUL JUST!	Lillian Beckwith	60p
☐	EVEREST THE HARD WAY	Chris Bonington	£1.25
☐	THE HISTORY MAN	Malcolm Bradbury	95p
☐	A RUMOR OF WAR	Philip Caputo	£1.25
☐	RAVEN	Shana Carrol	£1.50
☐	2001: A SPACE ODYSSEY	Arthur C. Clarke	95p
☐	SAM 7	Richard Cox	£1.25
☐	BILLION DOLLAR KILLING	Paul Erdman	95p
☐	ZULU DAWN	Cy Endfield	95p
☐	BLAKES 7	Trevor Hoyle	95p
☐	IN GALLANT COMPANY	Alexander Kent	95p
☐	CITY OF THE DEAD	Herbert Lieberman	£1.25
☐	THE VALHALLA EXCHANGE	Harry Patterson	80p
☐	SAVAGE SURRENDER	Natasha Peters	£1.60
☐	STRUMPET CITY	James Plunkett	£1.50
☐	SURFACE WITH DARING	Douglas Reeman	85p
☐	A DEMON IN MY VIEW	Ruth Rendell	65p
☐	THE SAVIOUR	Mark & Marvin Werlin	£1.25

Postage _____

Total _____

ARROW BOOKS, BOOKSERVICE BY POST, PO BOX 29, DOUGLAS, ISLE OF MAN, BRITISH ISLES

Please enclose a cheque or postal order made out to Arrow Books Limited for the amount due including 8p per book for postage and packing for orders within the UK and 10p for overseas orders.

Please print clearly

NAME ....

ADDRESS ....

....

Whilst every effort is made to keep prices down and to keep popular books in print. Arrow Books cannot guarantee that prices will be the same as those advertised here or that the books will be available.